As if I was a Real Boy

A single adopter and her adult son look back

GORDON AND JEANNIE MACKENZIE

BAAF
ADOPTION
FOSTERING

Published by
British Association for Adoption & Fostering
(BAAF)
Saffron House
6–10 Kirby Street
London EC1N 8TS
www.baaf.org.uk

Charity registration 275689 (England & Wales)
and SC039337 (Scotland)

© Gordon and Jeannie Mackenzie, 2011

British Library Cataloguing in Publication Data
A catalogue record for this book is available from
the British Library

ISBN 978 1 907585 24 1

Project management by Jo Francis, BAAF
Photograph on cover posed by models
Designed by Helen Joubert Designs
Typeset by Fravashi Aga
Printed in Great Britain by T J International
Trade distribution by Turnaround Publisher Services, Unit 3,
Olympia Trading Estate, Coburg Road, London N22 6TZ

BAAF is the leading UK-wide membership organisation for all
those concerned with adoption, fostering and child care issues.

Contents

Acknowledgements

We are extremely grateful to the following people who helped us in the writing of this book:

- Marie Scott, who gave us the original idea;
- staff at the British Association for Adoption and Fostering, who could see the potential for the book, and especially Florence Merredew for her valuable comments;
- Hedi Argent, our editor, for her wise advice on how to structure the story;
- Mary Monaghan, who has always retained an interest in her client and helped us fill in some of the gaps about Gordon's early childhood;
- Bernadette Mackenzie, David Mackenzie and Ted Milburn, who read our script and gave us encouragement and helpful suggestions for improvement.

Above all, we are grateful to each other! Working together on the script brought us closer together and confirmed all that we mean to one another.

About the authors

Gordon Mackenzie was born in Scotland and adopted in 1983 at the age of ten. He now lives in a small town in the Canadian prairies, where he works as a beekeeper in a commercial apiary. He has two children, three cats and plays a number of stringed instruments, including the mandolin. He plays guitar in the worship group in his local church and upholds his Scottish heritage by giving the Address to the Haggis at the annual Burns Supper.

Jeannie Mackenzie was born in Scotland and has no intention of leaving it. She has been a teacher and worked at a senior level in one of Scotland's leading education authorities. She has also researched and published in the field of education and is the author of *Family Learning: Engaging with parents*. She now teaches mindfulness approaches to help with stress and chronic pain. Much more importantly, she is Gordon's mum. Originally a single parent, she is now married with a blended family of three children and five grandchildren.

This book is dedicated to my children,
in the hope that it will help them
really understand their dad.

Gordon Mackenzie

The Our Story series

This book is part of BAAF's Our Story series, which explores adoption and fostering experiences as told by adoptive parents and foster carers.

Also available in the series:
- *An Adoption Diary* by Maria James
- *Flying Solo* by Julia Wise
- *In Black and White* by Nathalie Seymour
- *Adoption Undone* by Karen Carr
- *A Family Business* by Robert Marsden
- *Together in Time* by Ruth and Ed Royce
- *Take Two* by Laurel Ashton
- *Holding on and Hanging in* by Lorna Miles
- *Dale's Tale* by Helen Jayne
- *Frozen* by Mike Butcher
- *When Daisy met Tommy* by Jules Belle
- *Is it True you have Two Mums?* by Ruby Clay

The series editor

Hedi Argent is an independent family placement consultant, trainer and freelance writer. She is the author of *Find me a Family* (Souvenir Press, 1984), *Whatever Happened to Adam?* (BAAF, 1998), *Related by Adoption* (BAAF, 2004), *One of the Family* (BAAF, 2005), *Ten Top Tips for Placing Children in Permanent Families* (BAAF, 2006), *Josh and Jaz have Three Mums* (BAAF, 2007), *Ten Top Tips for Placing Siblings* (BAAF, 2008), and *Ten Top Tips for Supporting Kinship Placements* (BAAF, 2009). She is the co-author of *Taking Extra Care* (BAAF, 1997, with Ailee Kerrane) and *Dealing with Disruption* (BAAF, 2006, with Jeffrey Coleman), and the editor of *Keeping the Doors Open* (BAAF, 1988), *See You Soon* (BAAF, 1995), *Staying Connected* (BAAF, 2002), and *Models of Adoption Support* (BAAF, 2003). She has also written six illustrated booklets in the children's series published by BAAF: *What Happens in Court?* (2003, with Mary Lane), *What is Contact?* (2004), *What is a Disability?* (2004), *Life Story Work* (2005, with Shaila Shah), *What is Kinship Care?* (2007) and *Adopting a Brother or Sister* (2010).

Foreword

I can clearly remember all that happened to me way back, as if it were yesterday. There are so many confused emotions and feelings that it is hard for me to pin them all down, harder still to explain them to you, but I am going to give it my best shot.

My mum and I invite you to travel with us on a long journey. If you have experienced adoption, I think you will know that it can be a rocky road. Bear with us if the road seems to twist and turn a bit and the story seems tortuous at times – my life has never been straightforward!

I hope this book will give you some insight into how I came to terms with my past and the things that troubled me. I know you will be impressed by the courage of my mum who has stuck by me throughout. Most of all, I hope that if you are considering adoption, this book will give you the guts to go for it.

Gordon Mackenzie, 2011

1

A long journey home

JEANNIE

Ten minutes before we landed, the pilot announced the weather in Calgary was a little warmer than it had been when we left the airstrip at Lloydminster in rural Saskatchewan – with the wind chill factor, it was now only thirty degrees below. I had left my son's home the previous night, driving for an hour and staying in a hotel so I would be close to the little airstrip where I would catch the early morning flight, the only one scheduled for that day. I was already twelve hours into my journey and it would be another thirteen before I reached home.

The journey marked the end of a two-week Christmas visit to my son and grandchildren in Saskatchewan and I was keen to get back to a warmer climate, to my comfortable home in Scotland and most of all to my husband. When we landed, I found a café in a quiet corner of the transit terminal, ordered breakfast and powered up my laptop to catch up on my emails. During the time I had been in Canada, email had been my lifeline as the seven hour time difference made phone calls difficult. I was pleased to see that as well as loving messages from home, there was also one from my son, Gordon:

> Date: Monday, 29 December, 2008 7.44am
> From: Gordon
> To: Jeannie Mackenzie
> Subject: Have a good trip

Hi Mum

Hope the early morning start was not too much of a killer for you and I hope the rest of your long journey home is a good one. You make sure that you give that wonderful huggable man of yours an extra big special hug. You picked a good one there! I thank you for the words you said to me about the people in the community and how you said I had no need to hide in the shadows. I am going to take bold steps and stick my neck out and get out of the shadows of life and join the world. After all, my bipolar isn't who I am, it's only one bit of me. You left me with many good thoughts and a sense of hope again to fight another day. I enjoyed the deep in the guts talks and the laughs we had together. I was so bloody nervous before you came that you would judge me and come down hard on me. Yet you did not and for that I am truly thankful. I feel our relationship just got a whole lot stronger and that is something no one can take away from me. I am more and more sure I made the right move that spring day when I walked into the house and called you 'Mum' for the first time and stuck with you. It has not been easy at times, especially for you. Yet we are still together, mother and son.

Lots of love and miss you already

*Your son
Gordon*

Date: Monday, 29 December, 2008 9.15am
From: Jeannie
To: Gordon
Subject: Re: Have a good trip

Dear Gordon

What a lovely message to get, son! You cheered up your old mum's heart. I have never regretted the leap of faith I made when I decided to adopt you (before I even met you). As I said to you when we said goodbye last night, I am so proud of my son, and grow more so every day. Yes, there have been some rough times in the past, and there have been some wobbly moments in the last two weeks too, but I have always believed in you and I always will. It is hard as a parent to step back a bit and let your kid be independent, and I know I have struggled with that a little from time to time, especially when I see you do things that may hurt you or cause difficulties for you later on. Anyway, I find it easier to do as time goes on, now that I see you manage so many things so well on your own – and many of them better than I could!

I am sorry you were so worried before I came. If you have worries like that, never be scared to tell me about them. You know that I can take it straight. It is one of the best things about our relationship that we can always be honest with one another. Of course, there are many parts of your life that are nothing to do with me and I am happy not to know about them. I too loved our frank discussions. They were a great help to me in understanding what is going on for you and how you are growing in your ability to manage and to cope with things that would "turn a nun to prostitution", as your wicked old dad would say!

It was simply marvellous to spend these two weeks over Christmas with you and the children. You are a lovely dad. I know you find it hard managing to have them when you are on your own, but you get better at it all the time. They so love being with you and having their special times to talk and to play with you.

Take care, son, have a good day, and thanks once again for writing this lovely letter. I am going to keep it forever! Maybe we could use these emails when we write our book together!

Lots and lots of love
Mum

2

A real boy

GORDON

I had been taught that there was a God who listens to us and even though I did not think it would do any good, one night alone in my bed with everyone asleep, I asked for a mum. I prayed as children pray for things. I prayed like a child who has lost his best friend or a pet. I had no real understanding of what I was doing, but I had nothing to lose.

Well, the answer came swift and fast. So fast it took my breath away and left me dumbstruck. The next day one of my carers said to me, 'Gordon, there is a lady interested in meeting you and maybe being your new mum, how do you feel about that?' I really did not know how I felt about it. There was panic in me and sheer excitement all rolled into one. I mustered up as much courage as I could find and said I would like that a great deal. There was a small shadow of doubt, though. I had been down this road before. Part of me was ready for the feeling of emptiness that might come if my dream of a family came crashing to the ground again. Yet mixed with the fear there was also hope. The days leading up to meeting this lady seemed to drag on forever. I thought about it when I lay down at night and the first thing I thought about in the morning was what it would be like to be in a family again.

At last it was the night before the first meeting. I could hardly sleep at all and had to have someone hold me and reassure me it was going to be OK. It was far bigger than the night before Christmas and not knowing what Santa was going to bring next day! It was far more exciting than my birthday! Yet somehow I must have fallen asleep, because when I opened my eyes again the sun was shining in the window and I could hear birds singing. This was it! This was the beginning of the journey that would change the course of my life beyond what my childlike mind could ever imagine. I was scared to death and yet I felt courage rising in me. I thought this might be my last chance or that there might not be another chance for a long time. I was so nervous as I dressed in my best clothes and got myself all cleaned up. There was a buzz and smiles of encouragement from all the staff. I kept hearing people say, 'You'll be OK. It will work out! I believe this time it is for real.'

It was a beautiful day in spring and it would have been a great day to go off and chase bumblebees and catch tadpoles down at the pond. There was so much that could have been done if I had not had to go to this meeting, but I did not mind a bit. My social worker, Mrs Dunsmore, arrived in her car and was smiling at me. I loved Mrs Dunsmore. When she showed up it was freedom time – I'd go for a ride in her car and be treated as someone special. I felt she could see what I could become if I got half a chance. This time we did not go to the city. My new mum lived in a small town in the middle of farming country. As we drove through the fields, I kept wondering who this lady was, what she was like and, most importantly, why she wanted to adopt me.

Finally the car stopped at the house that was to become my new home. I really did not know what I would say to this lady or how to address her. Would I call her Miss or Mrs? Could I dare to call her Mum? The lady who came out of the house to meet us was tall and she had beautiful friendly brown eyes and long black hair, plus a big smile of welcome. Why would such a woman want to adopt me? I still did not know what to call her. So I just said the first thing that came to mind. 'Hi Mum!' That was the ticket that opened the door to her heart.

The first time I visited my new home I looked everywhere my eyes were allowed to go and I knew that this was the home for me. I knew the lady I had just called Mum would be that from now on. When she showed me the room that was to be mine, I kept saying, 'It's just as if I was a real boy!' It was as if I was a real boy who had a home and a family of his own. This was all new to me. There would be no one to have to fight for clothes or food. There would be no bullying here. This was a safe haven for me. I was terribly nervous but oddly at peace within.

I could hear the grown-ups talking, as grown-ups talk. I was sure it was about me. I heard small parts of their conversation and what I heard sounded as though I would be allowed to stay there. So I let them talk and enjoyed this new environment with so much that had still to be discovered. My new mum seemed to be someone I could trust. This was it. This was my family at last. Then the hard part came. All too soon it was time to go. I cried inside and my heart was yelling, 'No, please let me stay! I'll be good! I really promise I will be good!' My social worker promised me that I could come back and my new mum said she would see me soon. They explained to me that it would work best if I was more gradually introduced to my new home and family. I was still crying inside and I was mad. I wanted to shout out, 'I will make it work! I will! Let me out of this car! I will make it work. I don't want to go back. Please let me stay. I'll be oh so good!'

No one heard my cries inside and soon I was back in the

hospital. I never wanted to be there and now I wanted to be there even less. Was this a cruel joke they were playing on me? Was I to see my new mum again? How long would it be before I saw her again? I couldn't stop telling my carers all about the new lady who had become my mum. They assured me I would see her again soon.

The days were long and I found myself dreaming of what I would do with my new family. I thought of many things, but the most important thing was that my new home would be a safe place. It was so important to me to know I was safe, because too many times my safety had been on the line and I had to run from harm. I would hide under a bed or in a tree, anywhere to get away from harm. Safety was the most important thing. I felt safe at my new mum's place and wanted to go back for more. I could see there were hugs to be given there and love – not because it was my new mum's job, but because she wanted to love me. That is what makes this story so special. Mum chose me that spring day and I chose her. Most kids don't get to choose who they have for parents. In spite of the hard stuff, I was lucky to get to choose a new mum and family and eventually the day did come when I moved in for good.

JEANNIE

I was quite unprepared for the shock of recognition when I met Gordon for the first time. Of course, I recognised him from the photo albums and the video I had been shown, but this recognition was at a much deeper level – I felt as though I had known him all my life. He was not only instantly loveable, he was immediately someone I felt I could understand, with whom I could share feelings and dreams. I felt an overwhelming sense of responsibility for him; a drive to protect him and to nurture him. Friends have told me of "falling in love" with their babies when they are born – that instinct was as strong in me as it was in them, though this "baby" was a fully grown ten-year-old boy! I can only imagine how strange and terrifying it was to meet me for the first time, but he showed no sign of fear, he simply got out of his social worker's car and walked up the path, calling out, 'Hi Mum!' as he walked past me into the house.

When I showed Gordon the bedroom that was to be his, he cried out, 'It's just as if I was a real boy!' The bedroom was not that special – it was only a small bedroom in a tiny semi-detached bungalow and furnished very simply. When I was getting it ready for him, a friend suggested I let Gordon choose the duvet cover and curtains. Although I wanted to involve this new member of my family in making decisions of this kind, the room looked too bare and too institutional, too much like where he had come from. So I chose bright primary colours for the duvet cover and bought some toys and books. I made curtains from fabric that had simple pictures of farm animals and hung those on a bright red curtain pole. I could not have made a better choice – Gordon still has the curtains in his bedroom today, in spite of the fact that he is almost forty and lives four thousand miles away! Later on, he chose wallpaper – bright red with diagonal white stripes. It made me feel nauseous, but Gordon loved it.

Delighted as I was that Gordon liked his new bedroom, I was sad that he felt himself not to be a "real boy". What I knew already of the first ten years of his life made me understand why he regarded himself as different. He had suffered years of abuse and neglect in his family home, had been bullied in a children's home and locked up in a psychiatric hospital. Yet he had also experienced love within his birth family and had strong feelings for family members he had lost through death and separation. And there were staff within the care setting who had become important to him. It was a complex story, a twisted knot of incidents, experiences and people. From this snarled mess, Gordon was struggling to build some sense of who he was and where he belonged. I think it was when I heard his heartfelt cry about being a "real boy" that I decided that one of my top priorities would be to let him have as normal a life as possible. This wasn't going to be easy, as my own life had hardly been "normal"!

In the two years before Gordon became my son, I had been working with Barnardo's, the adoption agency that arranged his placement. I had gone through a thorough process of assessment, training and preparation to be an adoptive parent. I had discussed my own background in detail with the social workers and had felt, at times, that there was no dark corner of my life history that had not been exposed. I was thirty-two years old and thought I knew myself pretty well. Within a few weeks of Gordon's arrival, however, I began to accept that my own life story was much more complex than I had wanted to admit to Barnardo's. I too struggled with knowing who I was and where I belonged.

Mine was a two-parent family where I was the youngest of seven children. There was a great deal of love in our family, and our parents were highly supportive of our education and ambitions. I have a huge store of wonderful childhood memories and I adored my brothers and sisters. Our mother was an avid reader and gave us a love of literature, while our dad was an endless source of adventure and fun.

We were brought up on the tiny island of Eigg in the Scottish Hebrides, where we knew everyone. Our home had no electricity; it was lit with paraffin-fuelled lanterns called Tilley lamps. At bedtime, our mother would carry a lamp upstairs and sit it on the landing outside our bedroom doors. We undressed in the flickering shadows. Once we were in bed, she would read us stories till we drifted off to sleep. Long after we could read for ourselves, she continued to read to us and sometimes to tell us stories of her own childhood in Australia. Lying in the cosy darkness, without visual distractions, our imaginations were free to create our own images of the people and places she shared with us.

Our parents allowed us a great deal of freedom to play and experiment, and never seemed to mind too much if we made a mess or were noisy around the house. We had very few toys or games, but were allowed to create our own playthings from household objects, making tents out of bed sheets, drawing with chalks on the bare floorboards and staging plays and shows in theatres constructed from old curtains and broom handles. Our father often played with us and invented simple games to keep us amused on dark winter evenings. We were rarely indoors, however. Long hours were spent tunnelling in the long bracken, building dens and making arrows in the woods, paddling and building dams in the burn and wandering along the shore. Our parents never worried where we were – if they wanted us, Dad would come to the back door and whistle. Usually it meant a meal was ready, and we would leave behind the latest adventure and run home to be fed. It was an idyllic childhood, secure in every way.

When I was eight years old, we moved from Eigg to the city of Aberdeen. On the island, my brothers and sisters had been my friends and the whole island our playground. The city gave me my first experience of loneliness. We were cramped in a one-bedroom flat; the boys slept in the only bedroom, the girls in the living room, while our parents had a bed recess in the kitchen. In spite of living on top of one another, we began to move apart as a family – my brothers were making their own friends, and our parents enjoyed increased social contact and opportunities. I took longer to make friends and was bullied at school because my accent was different and I did not know how to play the ball games or sing the skipping songs. I was intimidated by the city girls with their smart shoes and brilliant white ankle socks. My socks were grey, and had already been worn by older siblings. I hated the restrictions of city life, with its strangers, crowded streets and busy traffic. I longed to be back on the island, to be playing in the woods.

My mother told me years later that these had been difficult times for her too. I was her last child and she had given birth to me when she was forty. By the time I was ten she was going through a difficult menopause. She was remote, and appeared uninterested in my life, probably because she was unwell herself. While she was in hospital having a hysterectomy, my oldest sister, who had a mental disability, was temporarily admitted to a care home. While there, she became very ill, lapsed into a coma and was not expected to survive. When she should have been recuperating, Mother had to divide her time between the younger children at home and my sister in hospital. Meanwhile, my behaviour gave the whole family cause for concern. I cried a lot and seemed to be very unhappy for no known reason. I had temper tantrums when I would lie on the floor or run out of the house screaming. I often tried to avoid school by claiming to be ill. At one point, my mother took me to the doctor who prescribed medication, probably diazepam, which was overprescribed in the 1950s, leading to serious problems of addiction. When my mother brought the pills home, my father threw them in the fire, for which I am eternally grateful.

Later, we moved back to the Hebrides. My father had been training to be a Church of Scotland minister while we were in Aberdeen and his first parish was on Islay. By now it was time for me to go to secondary school, which for all of us meant boarding on the mainland. The siblings nearest to me in age went to the state school, but I had a grant to attend a fee-paying boarding school in Edinburgh. When I was twelve years old, I left home at the beginning of September and did not return until Christmas. During this time, I had no visits from my family and was not allowed to speak to them on the phone. I got weekly letters from my father and occasional letters from my sister, but these did not provide enough reassurance that I was loved by my family. I fantasised that I had been sent away from home as a form of punishment for not being as well behaved as my siblings.

The school had been established for daughters of ministers, but we were outnumbered by the daughters of landed gentry, doctors and diplomats, who subsidised our cheaper places. I was ill at ease in this new social setting. My parents had not been able to afford a full school uniform and I stood out from the others by not having sufficient changes of shirts and socks to last a week. I secretly hand-washed my clothes and hung them up to dry overnight, an activity that for some reason was strictly forbidden. I found it hard to sleep in the large dormitory after lights were out, and would lie awake for hours missing my family, and worrying about the small details that were a daily challenge, such as how to find enough money to buy soap or toothpaste.

I found it hard to fit in with the new expectations, especially the demand for "ladylike" behaviour and the heavy emphasis on team sports. For me, the best part of school was the large library, which doubled as the senior common room. Juniors were only allowed to go there once a week, but I somehow persuaded the senior student in charge to turn a blind eye and allow me to borrow well over the weekly allowance of books. After lights out, I sat on the windowsill in my dorm, reading my way hungrily through classics, biographies and romances by the neon glow of the street lamp. In the end, I made myself popular by serialising "novels" I wrote on stolen school exercise books and by doing other students' English homework – I had sufficient imagination to write five different essays on the same topic and make them appear to be like someone else's work.

At the end of my first term, I was in a high state of excitement at the idea of going home after three-and-a-half months away from my family. I lay awake all night, sick and agitated. At last the time came to get up and catch the train to Glasgow. My father had had some business on the mainland and so he met me in Glasgow and we travelled home by plane together. Once we had landed on Islay, there was still an hour's drive to our house. As we drove, I rehearsed again in my mind how it would be when we got there. My mother would rush out to meet me and give me a big hug, just as my father had done earlier that morning. She would be amazed at how tall I had grown and would tell me how nice I looked, just as my father had done. Finally we reached the house. Although this day had already seemed to last forever, it was still only lunch-time and the rest of the family were out at school or at work. There was no sign of my mother on the doorstep as we drove up. I ran into the kitchen shouting out, 'I'm home at last!' My mother was bent over the stove, busy with the lunch preparation. She looked over my shoulder at my father and asked him if he had managed to get an important item from the mainland that she needed. He had not been able to find the item, and they then had a discussion about how they were going to manage without it. She did not look at me or speak to me. I went out into the back garden where I found the dog. He had only been a puppy when I left, now he was a fully-grown dog, but he seemed to know me and ran over to me, wagging his tail furiously. I buried my face in his long shaggy coat and whispered in his ear that it did not matter; I could get by on my own.

These childhood experiences made me tough and self-reliant. My independent nature may have been one of the reasons I felt I could adopt a child on my own. My tough outer shell hid a vulnerable centre, however. Part of my childhood had been taken from me too soon, and deep down I was very unsure of who I was. I had felt an outsider, a stranger in my own life since the day we left the island when I was eight years old. When I first got to know Gordon, I had not begun to acknowledge any of my own pain, but later I understood that one of the reasons I so strongly identified with him was that we had both experienced loss, and its effects still haunted us.

3

The making of a family

GORDON

The day had arrived when it was time to leave the place where I had been a prisoner for so long. It was time to go home with my new mum and really get going with being a family. I was glad to say goodbye to the children's home and glad to say goodbye to the hospital. Yet there were people there who were important to me. There was one man, Hugh, who seemed to stand out the most. He had taken me out from the children's home many times. Hugh was a big cuddly man with brown eyes who could see that there was more to me than some crazy, badly behaved kid. It was the same with my social worker, Mrs Dunsmore. There was a nurse too who saw "the something" in me; I loved the way she would cuddle me and make me feel loved and wanted.

To explain things properly, I need to go a bit further back to the beginning. I was on my way home from school that day when it happened. The details of the day stick in my memory, but over time the pain has dulled. I walked to my grandmother's house for tea and when I arrived there, I could see lots of cars parked outside and that seemed odd. If I had really known what was going to happen I would have run and run as hard as I could to get away. They told me I was going on a car ride. They never told me that this was goodbye to all I had ever known and goodbye to my family, toys and clothes. That was the day I was taken into care. I didn't know where they had taken my little brother and sisters. I could not tell people what was going on in my mind and heart, so I "acted out" and was very disruptive and aggressive to other kids and staff in the children's home. So then they placed me in a hospital, and I spent the next three years there, going back to the children's home every second weekend. I did not belong anywhere, and no one belonged to me any more.

So although I was sad to leave some of the people, I was glad to leave these two places where I had been so unhappy. My new mum came and picked me up and we were off for real this time. No games. No cruel joke. This was for real. I was going home. You may think that is the end of the story – but no, it is not over yet. There is way more to this journey! It would be nice if one minute you were a child in a children's home and the next, magically, you are a kid with a family and it was all smooth sailing. I'm afraid it's not like that. This is when the hard part comes. I was so used to life in institutions that I had forgotten what life was like being a kid with a family. I had to learn to understand in my head and heart that my new mum loved me and she really wanted me to stay. I had given so many people my trust in the past only to have the rug pulled from under my feet. My mum had to grit her teeth many times as I adjusted to this new life. I did some awful things and I tested the poor woman to the max. For the life of me, I don't understand why she put up with it.

It was hard for me to sleep alone in my new room. I was so used to sharing a big room with others sleeping nearby and to hear the sounds of them sleeping. It was hard for me to sleep in a new place and difficult to believe that there would be no more midnight rampages. In the hospital where I had been, there was always someone who got up after lights out and caused mayhem. It would not be long before there was a riot. Anything that was not bolted down became an object to be thrown. I would get worked up myself and become part of it. It was not because I cared about the riot – I was only protecting my own skin and fighting off attackers. The nurses just assumed that I was involved for the same reason as everyone else, but I was not. I was annoyed that my space was about to be invaded and my safety was at risk. So I received the same punishment as the others – sedation. It was a sharp feeling on my butt and then things got very hazy for a long time.

Before that there was the children's home. I could not sleep there either, for fear that my stuff would get pinched. The kids were a lot older than I was and anything they wanted was fair game for them. I did not have much, but what I had, I clung to for dear life. A special toy or a special piece of clothing, it did not matter what it was, I hung on to anything that made me feel I had some sort of life of my own.

So that is why the new room was so special to me and also so hard to get used to. There was nothing to endanger my space. It was tough for me to really get it into my head that this was my room and my mum wanted me to have it as my special place, because I was still working on the trust thing with her. But there was so much in the new room that was good.

First, there was the bed. This was no ordinary bed. This bed was made for me by my mum's own hands. It had wood slats in it and a piece of foam as a mattress. That bed was made just for me with love in every part of it. I probably drove my mum nuts because time and again she had to repair those slats when I broke them! That bed was so much more than just a place to sleep. Sometimes it became a rocket ship. Sometimes it became a racing car.

Then there were the times it became something to dive into to take cover from the wild creatures I imagined were after me.

Then there was the rest of my room. If you have been a small boy or are one right now, you will understand what a boy's room is to him. My room was protected by the force of Star Wars. I had tall creatures guarding the door of my room. They had swords and were ready at my bidding to slay anyone who might try to enter. I loved it. I could set up forts and know that they would still be there when I came back. I had insects in matchboxes and jars. I could set up my Lego and when I came home it would be just as I had left it.

Oh, how I wish I could tell you in words how important it was for me to have this room! Somewhere that was my own personal space. Personal space was something that I had always lacked. I could run into this room and it was far better than hiding under a bed or up a tree. I tried to fool myself many times that I could hide from my new mum; she let me be because she knew that sooner or later I would get hungry or need a hug. Mum knew that I needed to just be by myself sometimes. I started to really love my mum for letting me have the space to think about what was going on in my mind. Sometimes, of course, my mum had to come in to clean or bring me my laundry. I often looked at her as she entered my room and I could tell she was thinking, 'Good grief, what have we here now!' That smile and shake of Mum's head did not bother me, because it was different from other people in the past shaking their heads at me. This shake of the head was full of love and did me no harm at all. She helped me to decorate my room as I wished it to be. She didn't mind that I wanted crazy wallpaper and had funky ideas for furniture. Best of all were the cool curtains – they had pictures of black and white cows grazing calmly on green fields. I could picture myself down on the farm, driving a tractor and surrounded by cattle. The curtains were also made by Mum and I have them hanging in my bedroom to this day.

I loved the way I could stretch my imagination in my room and be anywhere in the world. I needed this space to heal and start becoming a boy again and not just someone who was trying to survive. Slowly I became a normal boy with my own family and my own home. My bedroom was somewhere that could reflect my personality and show people who I really was inside. My mum had many cool friends in the neighbourhood. Some of them were allowed into my safe haven, to look after me if my mum went out, to read me bedtime stories and sometimes even to join in my games. It was my way to show them that I trusted them.

Now I will trust you too as you read my story. I will let you enter my personal space and be a part of it.

JEANNIE

The Barnardo's agency that arranged the adoption for us in 1983 was called New Families. There is a wonderful sense of optimism in that title and it reflected my own sense of confidence about the undertaking. Gordon was not joining a family that was already in existence. It was not a family that had been together for several years with an established identity. It was not a family that already had children with whom Gordon would have to compete. It was a brand new family with Gordon at its centre.

Right from the start, Gordon felt our family was missing an important member.

'Can we have a dog?' he would plead.

'You have to take dogs for walks. Every day, even when it is raining.'

'But we like walking, Mum!'

'Dogs are really messy.'

'A bird wouldn't be messy. It would sing all day and catch flies!'

'You can't stroke a bird.'

'Can we have a cat?'

'Cats kill birds and we like birds.'

'Snakes are no bother at all! It would just be in its box in my room and you would never see it.'

'We are NOT having a snake!'

There was a long pause. I thought he had run out of steam, but I ought to have known better.

'Have you ever seen a Vietnamese pot-bellied pig?'

In the end, we agreed on a dog. We'd had dogs in my family and I knew what good companions they can be. I'd never trained a dog, so I read up on the subject before we brought our puppy home. I had laid down a lot of rules, one of which was that the puppy was never to be allowed in Gordon's bedroom. I made a list of tasks I expected Gordon to do – walking the dog before school, cleaning and filling her water dish, feeding her in the evening. I explained that he would have to be patient, as we had to find the puppy that would be just right for us – not too big (our house was tiny), definitely a bitch (they are easier to train) and not long-haired (our house was messy enough already). Typically, it was Gordon who spotted the advert in the window of our local vet's clinic. There were two border collie whippet cross bitches ready now and free to go to a good home. We went to see them and both of us fell straight away for the runt of the litter, a tiny bitch with traditional border collie markings, but thankfully with the short hair of a whippet. We drove home with her and I am not sure which one of us was more excited. 'Just remember', I warned, 'She is not to go in your bedroom. It's not hygienic. She is to stay in the kitchen until she is house trained.' I managed to keep her out of Gordon's bedroom for at least a week. One morning when I went in to wake him for school, I found the pair of them snuggling peacefully under the duvet, a small puddle and neat little poo discreetly parked on a piece of newspaper in the corner. I gave in. I learned early on that one of the keys to surviving parenthood is being able to tell which battles are worth fighting.

Susie proved to be just the right dog for our new family. She doted on Gordon and loved it when he took her for long walks. She helped him get to sleep at night and she was the perfect companion on a camping trip – there is nothing to compare with a warm dog in your sleeping bag on a cold night. She grew to be something of a "Munro-bagger", the term used for people who are obsessed with climbing all the Munros – the Scottish mountains over 3,000 feet. I've climbed a few, but Susie bagged many more with Gordon and other family friends. In spite of her short legs, she never seemed to tire. Sometimes, when things were really tough and I felt I could not confide in anyone else, I would tell her my worries and she would gaze at me soulfully as though she understood. Gordon would tell her his worries too – I would hear him talking to her long into the night. If that dog could type, she could have written this book!

The family we created through adoption had to develop a sense of who it was, which was somehow different from the sum of the people who made up the family. It needed customs, expectations and rituals, and all of these had to grow from scratch. This family had no history of its own, so each event would carry significance beyond the event itself.

Our first Christmas together was an example of how we created traditions. My recollections of Christmas in childhood were neither positive nor negative, but for Gordon the notion of Christmas was laden with unpleasant memories and a sense of bereavement. In the weeks leading up to Christmas, he became increasingly anxious and distressed. One day he would tell me he did not want any presents; the next he would complain in advance that he would not like any presents he was given. He made notices and hung them on the wall, announcing that Christmas was cancelled. Christmas cards would arrive for him from members of my extended family or from friends. Some of these contained gift vouchers for Gordon, who promptly tore them up. The closer it got to Christmas, the more distressing his behaviour became. He would slam doors and scream at me that I should tell everyone there were to be no more Christmases. I had arranged for one of my brothers and his family to spend Christmas Day with us, so that Gordon would have some playmates, and so that I would have some desperately needed adult company. As the day drew closer, I wondered if I should tell them not to come. It was hard enough to think of a bleak Christmas for us without ruining the festival for others.

The solution came to me during a sleepless night a week before Christmas. The following day, I waited until Gordon said once more that Christmas was to be cancelled. 'OK,' I said. 'I will cancel Christmas.' He looked at me in astonishment. 'You don't want to have Christmas, because you won't be with your birth family. You worry about it because it reminds you of horrible stuff that happened at Christmas. I don't really care about Christmas much either, so we will have just an ordinary day. Your cousins are coming to play with you, but they often come to play with you. It will just be an ordinary day. We will have turkey and a Christmas tree, but that will just be because your cousins will expect it – you and I will know it is just an ordinary day.'

'Will there be presents?' he wanted to know.

'Well, there will be presents for your cousins, because I have always given them presents and they will expect it. But I don't care if you don't give me a present.'

'But will I get presents?' he persisted.

'That's up to you,' I said. 'If you change your mind about Christmas, you will need to let me know in plenty of time before the shops close on Christmas Eve. Otherwise, there will be no presents; it will just be an ordinary day.'

Gordon is highly intelligent. He spotted the inconsistency in this immediately. 'What if other people send me presents?'

'Well, that is up to you too,' I replied, much more calmly than I felt, knowing how kind my family and friends had been already, contributing to a huge stack of hidden toys and games and books. I also strongly suspected that Gordon had found most of these gifts by now. 'If you change your mind and decide that you want there to be a Christmas, I am sure there will be presents from other people, but if not, I will just take whatever is sent to some poor children who don't have any presents, so they won't be wasted.'

'I don't care!' he said defiantly, 'No one will give me a Lego castle anyway!' To my great relief, he then ran out of the room, missing my smile as I congratulated myself on managing to get him the present I suspected he really wanted most of all – a Lego castle set, complete with jousting knights, a portcullis and drawbridge.

During the next two days, Gordon became more openly interested in the idea of Christmas.

'I know Christmas is just going to be an ordinary day,' he would say, 'But what sort of food will we have – I mean, for the cousins, of course?'

I got out recipe books and let him choose dishes and make shopping lists. He picked out a Christmas tree and enjoyed being allowed to help saw off the end of the stump so it would fit in a bucket. There were parties and special activities at school to enjoy and by Christmas Eve he was no longer talking of an ordinary day, but of what we would do on Christmas Day.

'Let's go shopping,' he said slyly, 'just in case there is something you have forgotten.'

We went to the shops and I managed to buy a few small extras for him, which he pretended not to notice.

Later we drove to the beach and took our dog for a walk along the shore in the twilight. The late afternoon was bitterly cold, but brightly lit by the sun setting over the snowcapped mountains of the island of Arran. Gordon was, and is, an excellent walking companion. At ten, he could easily outstrip children his own age, striding out deep in conversation. We walked a lot in those days, partly to give the dog exercise, partly because we both like walking, but mostly because it was a good way to calm him down and to talk about matters that might be more difficult to discuss while sitting at home. Gordon talked about the experiences that made him afraid of Christmas and I told him how I intended it would be in the future: a time when promises would be kept and he would be safe from fear. At the end of the walk, we decided that it would be a tradition in our new family for us always to have a walk together on Christmas Eve. We kept that tradition until Gordon grew up and left home.

One of the unwritten rules that developed in our new family was that no matter what Gordon had done, he could always tell me about it and we would sort it out together. I desperately wanted Gordon to have the real childhood he had missed: that included allowing him as much freedom to play as I felt was safe. However, I encouraged openness and most of the time Gordon would own up eventually. I had never found it easy to talk to my parents about anything difficult as a child, and there were lots of uncomfortable secrets that had troubled me. I was determined that Gordon would not carry that burden, so my approach was not to get obviously upset and angry when I found out that he had been naughty. "Naughty" is perhaps too mild a word for some of these misdemeanours.

One evening, Gordon had arranged to play next door, in his friend's house. Meanwhile, my neighbour thought her son was playing in our home. The boys had worked out this deception so that they would be free to climb the hill at the back of our estate in the dark. Earlier in the day they had spied a huge pile of logs that had been cut down from the mature woodland at the top. It was late October, and I imagine that Bonfire Night was in their minds (or at least in Gordon's mind, as I have no doubt whose were the brains behind this particular adventure).

The first indication that anything was wrong was when the two boys came home, filthy and flustered. They seemed anxious to talk about what would happen if someone phoned the fire brigade – would the police be told? Would the police know who made the call? Quickly, I worked out that there was a small fire somewhere and that Gordon and his little friend were responsible. Reluctantly, they told me that they had set fire to some sticks at the top of the hill. I was not that concerned, but after I had made sure the other little boy had got home safely, I walked to the end of our garden where I could get a good view of the hill. What I saw had me tearing quickly down the lane, across the level field, climbing over the barbed wire fence and sprinting up the steep incline. It was not until I reached the top that the full scale of the fire hit me. The pile of logs had been left under the trees from which they had been cut and the flames now leapt high into the air, risking the lower branches of the trees catching alight. Visions of the fire brigade being called, police involvement and hundreds of pounds worth of damage flooded through my mind. I would be seen as an inadequate, neglectful mother, letting her eleven-year-old child play out long after dark, with no idea where he was. 'Poor kid,' I could hear others saying, 'what do you expect? Single parent, no male role model, no wonder the kid turned out bad.' I determined instantly that I had to put this fire out myself before it was seen and before anyone called the emergency services.

My first task was to get to the fire. The field was home to a herd of bullocks that had circled at a respectful distance around the blaze. Perhaps they crowded around it out of curiosity or maybe they were just enjoying the heat.

At any rate, they had no intention of moving. I yelled at them, but they paid no attention. The flames were much more interesting. I grabbed a large branch and approached the herd menacingly. Still no movement. Reluctantly, I whacked one of the bullocks gently on its flank. Astonished, it jumped up, startling the rest of the herd. They did not retreat a great distance, but they parted sufficiently for me to get nearer to the fire. The heat was intense, but I grabbed large branches and pulled them away, rolling them in the dirt until the flames subsided. Each time I emerged from the heat bearing a huge flaming branch, the bullocks would stagger backward, then press in again. I felt as though I was the centre of some wild, primeval ritual.

For ages, I seemed to make no impression on the blaze, but gradually, when most of the larger logs had been dragged clear, I became aware that the blaze was not as fierce. When I finally felt it was safe to leave, I turned around astonished to find that no one else seemed to have noticed the fire. Below me, I could see our little peaceful estate. The doors of the houses were all closed and the windows all had curtains drawn. No one was out and about. I realised I had no idea where Gordon was. I tried to hurry home, but my legs were weak by now and it took me a long time stumbling in the darkness. I was shocked when I saw myself in the hall mirror. My feet were splattered with mud and manure, my face was blackened with soot and my sweater was ripped. The light was on in Gordon's room and he was curled up in bed, pretending to be asleep. There would be time tomorrow to have long talks about telling lies and the dangers of raising fires. For tonight, I was just glad we had escaped trouble with the police.

For years, Gordon has enjoyed hearing me retell the story of the fire and other similar tales. It reminds me of how much I enjoy it when I am together with my siblings and we say to each other, 'Do you remember the time when...?' There is so much security in having a shared memory.

4

Questions, questions, questions

GORDON

I used to have lots of questions in my mind. I wondered what I had done wrong to be taken away from my home. I had often escaped from the children's home and would sit in the bushes watching other families and wishing I was part of them, but a bit of me was scared of being in a family again. The memory of the violent things that had happened in my home would come back to me. I wondered if it was possible to be a family without the pain and without the violence.

In my birth family, I had two younger sisters and a younger brother, plus two older sisters who were adopted by another family when I was a baby. The reason I was not adopted at that time was that my grandparents offered to look after me and I stayed with them, until the younger ones were born. My life, before I was taken into care, was rough and very dangerous but not all bad. My dad could be fun to be with. He taught me boxing and to dance rock and roll style. He could help with my maths homework and took me rummaging for things at the dump. We had a fireplace in our home and I can look back now and treasure those times when he and I would go into the woods and have some man-to-man time collecting firewood. When he was drunk, however, he lost his caring, loving personality. There were times when I had to take the little ones and run for safety, knowing that Dad was in one of his drunken rages and that things were about to get very nasty at home. Often, in the middle of the night, my father would come bursting into the house after a bout of heavy drinking. He was not the kind of man who could just go and pass out on a couch and sleep it off. No – instead he would take his frustration with life out on my mum and there were nights when it was just not safe for me and my brother and sisters to be in the house. He could be a very violent man and anything that was not anchored down could become an object to throw or use as a weapon. One of his favourites was an axe.

When I was just five years old, I was already used to getting the little ones out of the ground floor window and carrying them down the back alley, heading for my grandparents' home, knowing we would be safe there. I loved my birth mother but she was under a lot of strain and it was difficult for her always to be around and to keep us safe. A lot of the time she wasn't there. I no longer blame her for that – I realise she had to get away for her own safety. I had to learn to look after the little ones, to change nappies and put the babies to bed. I cared for them while there was no one to care for me. So, in a sense, I went straight from being a baby into being an adult.

Much later, the social workers decided that we all needed to be taken into care. They thought I needed a family of my own, so I could let go of the responsibility for my younger siblings. I shed lots of tears about this, and had lots of questions. Being in a different family did not mean I could let them go. I still carried them around with me like a great weight on my shoulders. For a while, I knew where they were, and the two adoptive families used to meet up. Once, we went on a camping holiday together and I could spend time playing with my brother and sisters again. Then the family moved house and did not leave their new address. They disappeared and no one could find them.

JEANNIE

When he was quite young, Gordon would ask me continuously, 'Why did you want a boy?' I used to reply that I really liked boys. That answer seemed to satisfy him at first, but he kept returning to it as he grew older, each time wanting more detail.

'Why did you choose me?'

'Why did you adopt a boy, not a girl?'

'Why did you not have a baby?'

'What made you want to adopt?'

'Why didn't you get married?'

It would have been easier to answer Gordon's questions if I had been sure of the answers myself. I can't recall exactly where the impulse came from, or when precisely I decided to apply to adopt a child. Some of the answers probably lie deep in my own experience of family. My family was a little bit like elastic; there was always the possibility of stretching it to include someone else. In spite of the fact that there was so little money, our home was often full of other people. Some of them came for a cup of tea and stayed for a meal. Some of them came for a night and stayed for a month. We had one of those kitchen tables with an extra pull-out section – it was always possible to extend the table, set another place and dig up a few more potatoes for the pot. There were missionaries on home leave, aunts and cousins, lodgers and travelling salesmen. There were also homeless people, alcoholics and people whose families had broken up. There was always enough hot water for someone who needed a bath, and beds could be made up from chairs and sofas. It was just as well my mother was not house-proud and neither of my parents was precious about possessions. Their early married life, in the town of Clydebank, had taught them not to place much store on property.

In 1936, their first child was born, a bright and beautiful girl who caught meningitis in her infancy and was left with brain damage and severe epilepsy. A second child, my oldest brother, was born in 1938. On the nights of 13 and 14 March, 1941, Clydebank was the target of massive air raids which killed nearly 600 people and made 35,000 people homeless. My father was on duty with the Auxiliary Fire Service and my mother was in the shelter with the children. They escaped unharmed, but during the first night of bombing, their home took a direct hit and they lost everything but the clothes they were wearing. For many years, they lived in temporary accommodation. I think that the experience of homelessness and loss made them concentrate more on people than things and may have been one of the reasons that, wherever they lived, they felt they could always share that home with others. I am a long way from matching them in their lack of interest in material possessions, or the warmth of their hospitality, but I like to think that something of their quality and their spirit of service rubbed off on me. Certainly, they were instrumental in drawing me towards caring for a child who needed a family.

Most people would imagine that having six children would be quite enough, especially on a low income. However, when I was eleven, my parents decided to adopt another child, a girl of fourteen. Through a friend working in a children's home, they had heard of this young person who desperately needed a family and they made a rapid decision to adopt her. I adored having a sister nearer my own age, someone with whom I could share clothes and confidences. We moved shortly after she joined us and although I don't believe we tried in any way to cover up the fact that she was adopted, it was much easier for her to be accepted in a new neighbourhood, as we were all newcomers. So for me, the idea of building a family through adoption was established from an early age.

By the time I reached thirty, I had not met anyone with whom I wanted to raise a family. I had my own home, a good job and a full social life, but there was something missing. I had lots of nieces and nephews whom I adored and most of my close friends had children. I did a lot of babysitting and caring for other children, but I realised that working with children and "borrowing" them was not enough – I really wanted a child of my own. The idea of having a baby never occurred to me. Artificial insemination by donor was not widely available at that time and the faith community to which I belonged would have been very shocked if I had deliberately attempted to become pregnant outside marriage. More importantly, I had a strong feeling that I wanted to give a home to a child who was really needy and who had perhaps experienced difficulties in their early life.

Single parent adoption was becoming more acceptable in the early 1980s. It was even beginning to be recognised that a single parent, who has no partner or other children to compete for attention, could offer something special to older children who had experienced years of abuse or neglect and, in some cases, multiple placements in care homes and foster families. Being officially approved as a prospective adoptive parent took almost two years. Occasionally I was impatient, thinking wryly to myself that my exploits in my teens could so easily have led to me becoming pregnant without any such preparation! However, I respected the thorough procedure and recognised that I needed the time and support to think through my decision carefully, just as the agency needed to be sure of me. Meeting other single parent adopters was invaluable in strengthening my belief that this was something I could do.

Finally, I was invited to the agency's office to look through the profiles of children who needed families. I was shown into a private room, and left on my own to browse through a large file stuffed with the photographs and details of about forty children. I entered that room on a high, relieved to have arrived at this stage, but my first reaction to being given the folder was revulsion – not due to the children it described, but due to the notion of browsing through a catalogue in much the same way as one might browse for a new winter coat. These were all real children in need of a new home. To lump them together in a catalogue seemed obscene. How could I possibly choose between them? At first, I looked though the pages and was appalled that I had no emotional response to any one of the children. I told myself to stop panicking, but I reached the end of the folder knowing with certainty that I could not offer any of these children a home, yet their images haunted me. I felt as though I was the villain in some sentimental song, passing by an orphanage while children pressed their faces against the railings, appealing for me to take them home.

One of the staff came in to offer me a cup of tea and asked me how I was getting on. I explained how I was feeling and she said that I shouldn't get discouraged; they were receiving details of new children regularly. 'Actually, we've just got some information about one child – really hard to place and probably not for you. We don't have any photographs yet – would you like me to tell you about him?' I agreed, somewhat half-heartedly as I was feeling tired and emotionally drained. She started to tell me about a ten-year-old boy who was in a psychiatric hospital. She explained that he was being considered for adoption separately from his siblings as it was felt his needs were much greater than theirs and that he needed time with a parent on his own, although the plan was that he should have regular contact with his siblings. He hadn't been to normal day school for years and was significantly behind with his learning. She mentioned these issues hesitantly, as though she was sure they would put me off.

I still can't tell what it was that grabbed my attention and I am not sure it was anything that was said. All I know is that from the moment I heard about this boy, I knew I wanted to offer him a home and I felt I could make it work, as long as he felt it could work for him. I was relieved that my positive feelings were in the first place emotional rather than rational. Being led by one's emotions is probably not the best way to choose a car, but there is something calculating about choosing a child according to a list of criteria. The response came from somewhere deep in my gut. I was soon able to rationalise the decision – he was young enough for me to feel we had some chance of building a relationship before he reached his teens; he needed to be one-to-one with an adult and I could offer that. He needed help to catch up with his learning and I had the skills to support him. He needed to stay in contact with his siblings and I felt quite comfortable with that.

During the next few weeks, I was shown photographs and a video of Gordon and met the social worker who was handling his case. All the information I received confirmed my initial response and my only fear was that something would go wrong before the placement.

Sometimes, I have been asked if I would have acted differently had I known then what I know now. It is an impossible question to answer. Most of the big choices we make in life, we make without knowing how things will turn out. We marry, buy houses, choose careers and give birth to children with no certainty of the outcome. With almost half of the marriages in Britain predicted to end in divorce, it is surprising that we have the confidence to marry at all. For many years I was so caught up in the difficulties of raising my adopted family that I failed to notice that many parents experience heartbreak and disappointment with their birth children. But there is one thing I have always been sure of – I have never regretted adopting Gordon. He has brought incalculable richness to my life. I could not be the person I am today were it not for him.

Adopted children can't ever belong solely to their new families, no matter how unpleasant their early childhood experiences were, or how shadowy their recollections are. Outside their new family, there exists for them another family that carries their identity, their inherited characteristics and their shared reservoir of memories. If adoptive parents avoid speaking of their child's birth family, if they don't encourage questions and demonstrate respect for the importance of the birth family in their child's life, then the child may be forced to carry their fragile memories silently on their own.

Adopting an older child meant that there was no temptation for me to ignore Gordon's past, as I might have done had he been a baby. Nevertheless, I made a considered choice that I would encourage him to talk about his family and to ask questions about parts of his history he could not remember. I made it clear that it would never cause any difficulty between us should he want to contact them. Of course, children are not freed for adoption without very sound reasons. In Gordon's case, these reasons also meant that direct contact with his birth parents, while he was a child, was out of the question. Gordon never sought direct contact with either parent as a child, and he has never wanted to have any contact whatsoever with his birth father. However, when he was twelve, he told me he wanted to write to his birth mother. I was happy for him to do so and set up a system with the social work department, which meant that letters could be sent between Gordon and his birth mother without either of them knowing the other's address.

At first, Gordon was excited to hear from his birth mother. In her first letter she promised him a watch and some money with the next letter. The second letter never came, and at that point he was so frustrated that he didn't want to write to her again. It reminded him painfully of the promises that had been made to him when he was taken into care. The social workers said they were going to sit with him in the car for a while and then let him go back into the house – but they drove off with him and he never saw his family home again. His mother told him she would visit him in the children's home and bring his toys – but he never saw her again throughout his childhood.

I told Gordon to remember that although his mother had not been able to care for him and bring him up, she loved him very much. I believed that to be true – there was enough in the accounts that Gordon gave of his early life to know that it must be so. More importantly, I believed that Gordon needed to be able to hold onto the idea of a loving parent to strengthen his fragile emotional health and well-being. Gently, I explained that circumstances sometimes mean that people cannot keep the promises they fully intend to carry out. I suggested that his mother may have wanted to visit him, but have been prevented by the authorities. I explained it was likely that she had no idea where he had been taken.

Gordon has two older sisters who were adopted when he was a baby, and there was no further contact with this part of his family. His three younger siblings, who were taken into care at the same time as him, were placed for adoption with a two-parent family shortly after Gordon was placed with me. There were a number of meetings with social workers and the two sets of parents discussed how we would handle the children's contact with each other. I got on very well with the other parents, who seemed much more confident and competent than I was. We agreed to meet every six weeks or so, taking it in turns to meet in each other's homes. On one occasion we went on holiday to the same campsite together. The other family lived in their caravan while Gordon, Susie the dog and I lived in our tent. These meetings went well. The children loved being together and it was good to be able to have some adult conversation with like-minded people who shared this sibling group.

However, there were some tensions from the beginning. Gordon was keen to talk about the past with his siblings, while the other parents were understandably anxious that this might upset their younger children. When the families parted, Gordon was always distressed to leave his brothers and sisters; while they had each other, he was on his own again. I suspect it was also hard for him to let go of responsibility for the little ones; he had spent so long caring for them and worrying how they were. None of this showed in his behaviour, but I could sense throughout visits that he was like a coiled spring. Gaps between meetings grew longer. After about two years, the other family moved without leaving us their new address or phone number. I contacted the social work department, but they did not have the new address either. Gordon did not often speak about them and I did not pursue it. Although I was sad for Gordon's sake, I had to respect the rights of the other family to privacy.

5

No family is an island

GORDON

What is a family? Some say that it's a group of people who share their genes, and I guess that is true. Yet for me, family is a little more complex. Yes, I have family who share my genes, but there are also people who are no less my family even if they don't share my genes. A friend once told me that a family is a group of people who stick with each other no matter what happens.

In the children's home there was no one I really could call family, just well-meaning staff who tried their best to fill the gap. Yet as hard as they tried, it was not enough to fill the void in my heart or to answer the cry of my inner being to belong somewhere. I would go and hide in trees, and watch families going to church on a Sunday, thinking, 'I wish that was me, oh how I wish that was me.' My birth family took me to church and I yearned to do that again.

When the door finally opened for me to have a family again, that family was not only the people who were part of my mum's family. Others got roped in to become family for me. An older couple who were friends of my mum's became like grandparents. My mum seemed to trust them and so I felt I could too. Mr Scott took me under his wing and taught me things about nature and the world. Mrs Scott played the piano; my interest in music was sparked by this lady and it is still a very big part of my life. My new mum had a friend who was also single and I came to know her as my Aunt Frances, although I was no relation to her at all. I could fill pages and pages with the adventures I had with Aunt Frances! Without a shadow of doubt, she was someone I knew I could trust. She was someone I could share the innermost parts of my being with and someone I could ask just about every question one can possibly imagine. Questions about life, climbing, camping and there were no holds barred to talking about bodily functions! She made me laugh out loud asking me how many hairs I had under my armpit and looking for hairs on my chin. My mum needed a break from time to time as I had more energy than most. Aunt Frances had a way to get the wriggles right out of me, taking me up mountains and camping on hillsides with her friends.

I so badly needed to belong and know that there were people who cared for me, not because caring was their job, but because it was what they wanted to do. In the beginning I would search to find out if there was a hidden motive behind this love and willingness to be part of my life. I would give them a hard time to see if they would get fed up with me and walk away. Now that I'm an adult, I regret driving people to distraction, and yet I had to test them out to see if it was for real. So many times in the past I had been let down and left to lick my wounds; left to think that I was a mistake and really did not belong on the planet at all.

Now I sit here as an adult and chuckle a little to myself. Many people have struggled to understand what I call my family. I have my birth family, my mum's family, my new dad's family, my in-laws in Canada and other friends, close friends, who are like family to me.

JEANNIE

Any family finds it hard to exist without a network of friends. I worked full-time as a teacher while Gordon was a child and was fortunate in having good friends who would mind him in the short period between school and the time I finished work. Marie and John Scott had been my sponsors during the adoption process and they became like grandparents to Gordon, their large house becoming a second home for both of us. When times were tough, their home was a refuge. I would sit by the Aga in their lovely warm kitchen and talk with Marie while John would find some outdoor task which would calm Gordon down. John had a deep empathy with Gordon and they would work away together happily with hardly a word spoken between them. John usually had a project on the go and he was always happy for Gordon to get involved. Their house was at the start of a local nature trail that led through a wooded gorge. One project involved growing young oak trees to nurture and plant out alongside the trail. Gordon became engrossed in that activity, scouring the countryside to find the healthiest acorns for the tree nursery in John's garden. The saplings they grew are now large trees, and on a recent visit to Scotland, Gordon proudly showed them to his own children.

Gordon has always loved animals. Shortly after he started going regularly to John and Marie's house, their cat had kittens. One day Gordon decided to bathe the kittens. Understandably, neither the kittens nor their mother enjoyed the experience and their protests alerted the adults to what was happening. The kittens were ruffled, but had come to no real harm. Gordon was given a mild telling-off and ran away. When I came to pick him up, he could not be found. I returned home, expecting that he would eventually appear. I was preparing a meal in the kitchen when I spotted him through the open kitchen window, hiding in the bushes. To my horror, he held a broken milk

41

bottle in his hand, and looked as though he meant to use it as a weapon. I kept on peeling the potatoes, pretending not to see him while I wondered what to do. It was reasonable to imagine he might feel guilty for harming the kittens and scared that I might punish him. That he believed he might have to defend himself with a broken milk bottle was much more puzzling. What kind of punishments had he suffered in the past that would make him so afraid? I struggled to appear calm, remarking casually that he ought to make sure his hands were washed before he came in for his favourite meal of sausages and chips. A few moments later, he came in without the bottle, washed his hands and sat down to eat, while still eyeing me warily. I gently let him know that I knew about the kittens, but that I could not imagine he had really meant to harm them. He visibly relaxed and we were able to talk properly about how important it was to handle all animals with great care, especially helpless little ones.

Later that evening, he wrote a note of apology and we drove to John and Marie's to deliver it. I knew it was important for him to return to the house that day, or he would be afraid to go back. It was the first step towards him understanding that I did not believe in physical punishment, but preferred making amends and talking through what had happened so that he could better understand where he had gone wrong. It was also an important step towards him developing trust, not only in me, but in John and Marie as well.

Friendships worked particularly well when they combined interests for both Gordon and me. I had a colleague who was also a single parent and was bringing up three children on her own. It is much easier to ask someone to mind your child, or take them to a hospital appointment, when you know that you can help them out in turn. Liz and I supported one another with everyday tasks, but also emotionally. On Friday evenings I would take all four children for a swim while Liz fetched a fish supper for us all to share. The kids would settle down to watch a movie and Liz and I could have some adult talk in the kitchen. She has a wicked sense of humour and we would spend a lot of time laughing, a great relief from the daily grind of managing work and children.

Her wise counsel was particularly helpful one day in the first summer Gordon was with me. He had taken to threatening to run away. He would pack a bag, leave the house and wait for me to come and find him. At first I would talk to him about why he wanted to go, but then I switched to a new tack. Assuming that his actions were attention-seeking behaviour, I judged that the less attention I gave him, the sooner he would stop. Liz called one day when he was threatening to pack his bag once more. I was very tired and frustrated by his behaviour. 'On you go then!' I said, 'The quicker the better!' He went to his bedroom and stumbled about muttering to himself. I explained to Liz why I was acting in this way. She said nothing for a while, but then, as Gordon left the house, slamming the door, she stood up and said that if I did not bring him back, she would. 'He needs to know that you will never let him go.'

I went after Gordon and found him standing in the middle of the field. He ran away as he saw me arrive, but I ran after him and caught him in my arms. I lifted him up and carried him back to the house like a baby, while he screamed and howled that he wanted to run away. Although Gordon was only ten, he was strong and fast, and there was no way I could have caught him or carried him if he had been serious about resisting, and I drew some comfort from that fact. I dumped him on his bed, and hugged him very tight. 'I am not ever going to let you run away,' I said firmly. 'You are my son now and I am your mum. I don't care whether you hate me or not. This is your home and you are going to stay in it, like it or not. So just get used to it.' After a while, he calmed down and let me cuddle him and then we unpacked his bag together. I left him playing and returned to the living room to speak to Liz, but found she had wisely slipped out and left us to ourselves.

There were a number of people who were prepared to take Gordon for a night or two to give me a break. The one he liked to be with most was Frances, a friend of mine who appears to have boundless energy and enthusiasm for adventure. She took him skiing, climbing and camping and was willing to take Susie, the dog, along too. She works with troubled children and had a great understanding of Gordon, and could tease him out of a bad mood. I never worried about Gordon's behaviour when he was with her; I knew she was more than able to cope. She can be very blunt – Gordon adored her frank talking about bodily functions.

I am a reasonably active person. I like to be busy and can work long hours and still be ready to party. However, my son's seemingly inexhaustible store of energy soon wore me out. He appeared to need constant activity and was often deeply engaged in some project that would come before everything else. He had high, frequently unrealistic expectations of what he could achieve. One example was his desire to sew clothes for his tiny Star Wars figures. I am a passable seamstress, but making garments on that scale was beyond me. Yet Gordon would beg for scraps of fabric, needles and thread and sit up in bed attempting to create vests and jackets for the smallest figure, Yoda, an old wizened creature, less than an inch high, with a wise and kindly smile. This would continue long past bedtime, and often I would give in and go to sleep myself, waking in the small hours to find him still at it. In spite of these late nights, he was always up and ready for school the next morning and rarely appeared to be tired. Sleep did not come easily to him, and this caused tension between us, as no matter how patient and considerate I could be during the day, when it came to being deprived of sleep myself I could get very crabby indeed. Having friends who could give me breaks from time to time, so I could catch up on sleep and recharge my batteries, was very important for me.

After Gordon had been with me for about three years, we moved to a larger house and I was able to respond positively when a young friend asked if she could lodge with us for a while. We had worked together and she was now returning to university for post-graduate study. Having Anthea as part of our family, albeit temporarily, took a great deal of strain from me. An outdoor enthusiast, she involved Gordon in daily jogging and took him canoeing and mountaineering. She acted like an older sister: she was available for advice and support, but very wisely stayed clear of discipline and parenting issues. Her presence brought other young people into the house and our home became a hub of youthful activity. I liked it that way – it was more like the home I had grown up in, always busy and lively.

My own family played a generous role in supporting us. Holidays were much easier when shared with my brothers and their families. My brothers were very positive role models for Gordon and provided the rough and tumble play that he enjoyed. Of course, I baby-sat for them and supported them too, but I received much more than I ever gave in return. My sister lived too far away to be actively involved, but she was a willing ear at the end of the phone, and, having been adopted by my parents when she was fourteen, she could give me some insight into Gordon's feelings.

When I adopted Gordon I hoped that my parents would be able to spend time with him. His birth grandparents had been very special to him, but they had both died not long after he was taken into care. My parents had thirteen other grandchildren, but distance meant that they did not see much of them – I wanted things to be different for Gordon. Being adoptive parents themselves, they accepted the idea that I wanted to adopt without a qualm. Gordon hit it off particularly well with my dad – he had once been a joiner, and he got involved enthusiastically with Gordon's projects, making a table for his model railway set and a rabbit hutch. (If I had thought Gordon was going to be satisfied with a dog, I was wrong – the dog was just the first in a long series of hamsters, guinea pigs, stick insects and rabbits!)

We used to visit my parents regularly, but it was a four-hour round trip, so it was wonderful when they moved into a house a few streets away, when Gordon was about fifteen. My mum had not been well and my dad needed more support. Gordon's very caring nature meant that they were regularly visited, and there was a strong young body around to help when any heavy work needed to be done.

Dad and Gordon had a lot in common in their approach to life – if I did not know better, I might be convinced Gordon had inherited some traits from him. They shared a preference for action over anything sedentary. With both of them, it was impossible to make a suggestion that we do something without going from plan to action at a speed that left the rest of us breathless. They were both more likely to take a running jump to clear a fence rather than walk a bit further along to find a gate. If you were to ask either of them for help with a task, the job would be done almost before you had finished the sentence. From the moment they met, I think they sensed a kindred spirit. At any rate, a wonderful relationship was established. Towards the end of his life, my father developed dementia and lost touch with a lot that was happening, but whenever I visited, he would emerge from the fog long enough to ask, 'How's that big boy of yours?'

6

What's wrong with me?

GORDON

For so long, I sensed something was wrong with me. I could not pinpoint what it was. Often I was so frustrated trying to work it out that I behaved badly. I screamed inside and wished I could let other people reach into my mind and let them know what was happening with me. Yet I could not do that. I was like a newborn baby that can't tell its mother what it wants. My mind was heavy at times and then everything was all cloudy and unclear. I felt great anger one moment, and great sadness the next. My mind was something I could not control. I tried so hard to figure out how to make my mind be at peace, but I could not. I could not understand why I was having so many problems inside my head at times. I finally had a good family, a loving mum, a good home and life was secure. Why did I keep on feeling like this?

It was not till I was an adult that I finally had the answer.

JEANNIE

I knew before I met Gordon that he had been identified as

having some psychiatric problems, but I was optimistic, believing that his distress could be easily explained by the trauma he had experienced, and that a steady, loving and supportive home environment would help him recover. When the introductions were at an end, the social worker suggested I collect Gordon from the psychiatric unit where he had spent most of his time, so that I would have an understanding of his life there. On previous visits, he had been brought to my home or I had collected him from the children's home. When I arrived at the hospital, Gordon was waiting impatiently inside while the staff unlocked the door. 'It's OK, Mum,' he said. 'They just keep this door locked because the little ones might run into the road.'

The building that was so carefully locked was set in parkland, some distance from any traffic, so I knew his words were a polite fiction, masking the embarrassment he felt at being an inmate of a locked ward for children with mental health issues. The parkland surrounded a large Victorian psychiatric hospital. The social workers had told me that Gordon had been referred to the hospital shortly after being taken into care. Staff in the children's home had become concerned about his safety as he had been found several times on the railway line near the children's home. It was not clear if he was attempting suicide, but there was no doubt that he had been in a very distressed state.

I was shocked by what I saw inside the locked ward. This institution was effectively the only home Gordon had – he spent every second weekend at the children's home, but was incarcerated here for the rest of the time. The ward consisted of a large, long room with two rows of five beds lining the sides. In an attempt to make it more child-friendly, some Disney characters had been painted on the walls and in one corner there was a soft play area, but nothing could disguise the fact that this was a hospital. A connecting corridor led to the small schoolroom where Gordon had received his only education since being excluded from school five years previously. There was no time to take in the details, as Gordon was keen to get out of there as quickly as possible. This was the day when he was coming home with me for good. No more introductions, no more visits – this was the real thing. One detail did not escape me, however. Gordon was medicated. His pupils were dilated and he seemed sluggish compared to the last time I had seen him, when I collected him from the children's home.

During the early months of the adoption, I still believed that whatever behaviour had caused the authorities to lock him up and drug him was likely to disappear once he settled into a normal home life. Gordon seemed happy and appeared to adapt relatively easily to attending a real primary school. He made friends with other children in our street and played outside in the long summer evenings on his new bike. He was enthusiastic about the new people he met and about a range of new experiences. Like me, Gordon loved the outdoor life, camping, lighting fires on beaches and climbing hills. He acted responsibly with our dog, Susie, taking her for a walk and feeding her every morning before school. He was affectionate and loved being cuddled and having bedtime stories. He often told me how much he liked his new home and there was never any doubt that he wanted me to be his mum. Car rides and country walks were great occasions for long conversations – Gordon had an insatiable appetite for knowledge and he questioned me constantly, particularly about nature and technology. I discovered he had a great sense of humour; we were often laughing, and we enjoyed one another's company.

Gordon moved in at the end of May, and early in July we went on holiday for a fortnight with two of my brothers and their families to a croft on the island of Skye. I was working full time as a teacher and was looking forward to a six-week break and to having more time with my new son.

I realised that I had been tense during the last two months, anxious to be the perfect mum and feeling the strain of being the only adult responsible for Gordon. Gordon loved his new uncles, aunts and cousins and I relaxed with the support of the extended family. We had fun training our new puppy, going for long walks along the beaches, building fires and fishing for mackerel off the rocks. The children played happily together outside the croft, building dens and sliding down the grassy slope in disused fish boxes. I loved being able to give Gordon this freedom and share with him some of the joy of my own childhood.

The idyll came to an abrupt end when we returned home. On the first evening back, some of the local kids came around to play, as usual. Gordon took a box of toys into our garden and shared them with the others. All seemed well until I heard a high pitched screaming. Thinking someone had been hurt, I ran out to find Gordon throwing his toys at the other children and shrieking at them to take the toys away. The other kids were startled and most of them were already running away by the time I arrived. Gordon was rigid, his eyes were fixed and glazed and he did not seem to hear or see me. He ran into the house and began breaking up toys in his bedroom, putting some in the bin and stamping on others. All the time he muttered to himself, 'Right, let's get on with this, and let's get this done.' Once he had destroyed his most treasured possessions, he seemed to calm down, but was still talking to himself. 'OK, that's that sorted, let's get on,' and he became engaged in watching cartoons on television. When I spoke to him, he did not appear to hear me, and I was unable to reach him to talk about what had happened.

This episode was followed by another similar one a few days later and all summer long I struggled to deal with this bewildering behaviour. Sometimes he destroyed his toys; sometimes he was self-destructive, repeatedly banging his head on the wall. Before I met Gordon, I had worked for six years in a residential school for children with emotional and behavioural difficulties. Some of the children could be aggressive and self-harm, but I discovered that it was quite different dealing with those issues in my own home. I thought I had had a very thorough preparation for adoption, but no one had mentioned that what hurts your adopted child hurts you more. It seems blindingly obvious now, but nothing had prepared me for the gut-wrenching feeling I had every time Gordon was upset. If I could have taken away his pain and had it myself I would have been much happier. It dawned on me that this is what it meant to love your child.

If there was a trigger for his wild behaviour that first time, I could not find it, and Gordon was quite uninterested in talking about his distress, even after he had calmed down. It seemed as though the event had happened in some other realm, to someone else. The most frightening aspect for me (and, I suspect, for Gordon) was the apparent presence of another person Gordon would speak to while he was having an attack. There were also times when he did not physically act out, but was clearly aware of another presence and stared fixedly at a person he believed to be there. At these times, it was possible to sit with him, hold him and reassure him that there was no one, and that he was quite safe. He would then respond to me and let himself be held and cuddled. However, when an episode became more physical, any intervention on my part appeared to make it worse for Gordon. He seemed to have an illusion that I was someone else, someone of whom he was afraid. Attempts to restrain him, even by gentle holding and reassurance, were treated with more intense violence. In spite of this, our relationship developed and became stronger. I clung to the hope that as he became more secure with me and the memories of past troubles faded, so too would these strange and violent episodes.

At this stage, we still had regular visits from the social

workers who had originally arranged for me to foster Gordon with a view to adoption. I never had any doubt that I wanted to adopt Gordon, but regulations meant that I had to foster him for six months before I could apply to adopt. I noted that Gordon would get anxious before every visit from the social worker. He was afraid I would talk about how difficult he was and that he would be taken away from his new home. I was also anxious, afraid that admitting to not being able to handle his behaviour would mark me out as an unsuitable adopter. Asked by the social workers how we felt he was settling in, both of us were probably more positive in our accounts than the facts justified. However, I was not always able to hold back. One Saturday night when I felt I could not cope, I called the duty social worker. I had no clear idea what I was looking for, but once I knew she was on her way, I panicked in case my admission of needing help might lead to the placement breaking down. Instead, the social worker who arrived handled the situation extraordinarily well, calmed us both down and left me with some practical suggestion for coping.

Gordon returned to school at the end of our first summer together. He was not long back before the head teacher called me, concerned that Gordon had been distressed in school that morning. Involved in some minor misdemeanour, he has been sent to see the head teacher, but had alarmed the staff who were escorting him along the corridor by screaming that there were too many doors in the school.

A few days later, some of the children told their teacher that Gordon had attempted to hang himself in the school toilets using his school tie and I was summoned to the school again. The head teacher suggested that maybe a special school would suit Gordon better. My heart sank. During the period when I was being introduced to Gordon, the professionals involved had recommended the local school for pupils with "moderate learning difficulties". However, there was something about his advanced language development that had made me argue for a mainstream placement. He had begun to make significant progress in his first few months, so the suggestion that he now be placed in a school where there would be lower expectations and less stimulus filled me with dread.

I insisted that Gordon remain at the school and I met with his class teacher to discuss the strategies that I had begun to develop in order to deal with his strange episodes. These included providing him with more space when he became agitated, for example, by allowing him to be on his own, perhaps to take a short walk. The incident when he had attempted to hang himself was due to bullying, and the school promised to be more alert. I was thinking on my feet at that point, not sure myself what would work best. I was also uncomfortably aware that what might work in our home environment might not be possible in school. However, the staff at the school were wonderful – they were prepared to accept a lot of difficulties and were good at explaining to the other children that sometimes Gordon might have to be treated differently. Much of that positive response was due to Gordon himself. He had such a likeable nature, which more than made up for the problems he caused. Fortunately, the more extreme incidents of strange behaviour were confined to our home. At first, that made me feel very low indeed. I wondered if somehow I was not handling him properly, but in time I realised that it was because he felt safe with me that he could allow me to see his more troubled side.

As the autumn wore on, the attacks became less frequent and there was a long period of calm. I felt confident that the security of his new home life was making an impact. However, a few months later, the violent episodes began again, and this pattern continued. Each time there was a lull, I believed the attacks would not return, and each time I was proven wrong. As he got older, some aspects changed, but three features were constant: during an attack, Gordon would be unreachable, apparently oblivious to anyone around him. He would talk rapidly to himself, sometimes under his breath. Finally, most incidents involved violence which he appeared not to remember afterwards, and for which he never showed any sign of remorse.

In addition to the attacks, there was also self-harming and suicidal behaviour in his teenage years. On at least one occasion he cut himself and once he took aspirin from the bathroom cabinet. I consulted the social worker, our family doctor and the school psychologist, but none of these professionals seemed particularly alarmed, nor were they able to offer help, other than a referral to a psychiatrist. The waiting lists were long and I was very reluctant to have Gordon referred. He had been in a residential psychiatric facility for four years and it did not appear to have done him much good. There seemed to be perfectly understandable reasons why he should be distressed from time to time. So while his general development continued to progress, I avoided any action which might have taken him on a route back into psychiatric care of any kind. He desperately needed to lead as normal a life as possible.

7

Every day's a school day

GORDON

I had very little time in the regular school system. In my early childhood I found school a hard place to be and I just did not fit in with most of the kids there. They had fairly peaceful and normal family lives and I had troubles at home that would not leave me even when I went to school. Most days, I went to school hungry and tired. My grandparents were both deaf and because I spent so much time with them, I rarely spoke and mostly used hand signals to convey what I wanted. That made it difficult for me to learn to read and write.

When I was taken into care, things just got steadily worse with my schooling. I had a pile of problems that would have made most kids say, 'Stuff it – there is no point in trying!' I didn't know it at the time, but I was deaf in one ear and dyslexic. All this was on top of worrying about my family and being picked on by the older kids in the children's home. I'd had to fight to find my place in the pecking order there. I tried regular school but children can be so cruel when a kid does not fit in to what they class as "normal". I was shy and like a scared rabbit most of the time. I was always looking over my shoulder and always ready to run from danger at the drop of a hat. Plus, I had something wrong in my mind that I could not figure out.

If I was confused, that was nothing compared to the staff in the children's home. They had no idea how to help me with my learning. The hospital had its own classroom, but it was not like a real school. The teachers were gentle but they did not expect much from us and I did not make much progress there.

Yet the odds suddenly tipped in my favour when my mum adopted me. Learning was still hard for me, but I finally had something worthwhile to make me want to learn. I had my new home and my wonderful bedroom. Many times when I was having a hard day at school, I would grit my teeth and dream of what new adventures I could have in my room and what unfinished projects needed my attention once I got back to my little world again. I also knew that there was a warm hug and a shoulder to cry on when things got too tough at school. That was the answer to a good deal of problems in my life. To know there would always be a good meal and a good night's rest in a place where things would not go "sideways" in the night. There was no drunken father to come crashing through the door and no big bullies to try and steal my stuff.

My new mum was a teacher and had experience dealing with kids who had a troubled home life and difficulties at school. She was able to talk to my teachers on their level and discuss how to help me regain the ground I had lost in my early days. But I still had my part to do in all of this and there were still mean kids who picked me out as the playground oddball. I was determined to find a way round this problem of being the oddball, so I made friends with as many boys and girls as I could. There was safety in being with a group; on my own I was easy pickings for the kids who were looking to make someone's life a misery.

My mum being a teacher, it also meant that she could unlock the door to me finding my path to knowledge, and once that door was unlocked my world changed forever. I wasn't just learning stuff – I was learning how to learn, and I still have those skills as an adult.

I found out that learning could be fun. This was a concept that took a while to sink in. My mum found many ways to teach me outside of school, like going for walks so we could learn about nature. She never minded if I made collections of things like leaves, nuts or, worse, beetles and worms. My bedroom was a mess at times, but she didn't worry too much about that. Then there was going shopping with my mum for groceries, and looking at the price of things on the shelves, and working out what would fit into the weekly budget. I was learning maths without even knowing I was. That was the key for me – to learn without knowing that I was learning. If she had treated it like schoolwork, I would have been afraid and would have backed off right away. I had a fear of learning because I knew if I didn't get it right, I would be judged as daft and would be made fun of. I was so used to failing in class and getting poor marks.

My mum had friends who were teachers too, and some of them also found ways to teach me without me really knowing I was learning. And most of my new teachers at school were fun. I could tell right away if a teacher was doing their job just because it was a job, or because they loved teaching and wanted to be there. I was drawn to the teachers who loved what they were doing. They became part of my world.

To this day, I will not attempt to explain the way I learned to understand maths. The way the teachers explained it made no sense to me, so I developed my own techniques. When my marks in tests were good, they accepted my weird methods. They continued to teach their way, and I continued to give maths my own twist and make it fit into my way of learning. I caught up quickly and soon I was much the same as every other kid; in some cases I had better marks than they did.

JEANNIE

The way in which children learn outside the formal classroom setting intrigues me. I have worked in and around schools throughout my career, but it took me some time to wake up to the potential of the home as a learning environment. I started out as a primary school teacher in the early 1970s, not long out of the classroom myself. My first school was set in a small village in a mining area in Fife. The village had expanded in the earlier part of that century to accommodate miners who worked in the colliery, but as the colliery had long since closed, unemployment was high. Like all the other teachers working there at the time, I travelled into the village from some distance and had almost nothing to do with the families or the community. Parents came once a year to hear about their child's progress, and we only saw them at other times if there was trouble.

Later, I worked in a residential school for children who had emotional and behavioural problems, and was even more remote from the parents of my pupils until a social worker attached to the school invited me to join her in running a group for the parents. I had tended to see parents as part of the problem, rather than part of the solution. That evening, for the first time, I listened to the parents' perspective and was humbled by their knowledge and understanding of the issues that affected their children, and of the role they were playing in their children's education. Although I continued to teach for several more years, it was at that point that I began to be drawn to including parents in my work. While I learned a great deal about parental involvement in the work context, it was becoming a parent myself that made the biggest impact on my understanding.

When Gordon came to me at ten years old, he struggled to read and write. He could not tie his laces or tell the time and he had some difficulty dressing himself. Yet within a year, he was not only able to do all of this, he was also reading at the same level as his peers. He had excellent teachers and specialist support, but the learning at home had an important part to play. I reasoned that motivation to read was as important as the reading skills he was being taught at school, so I set out to encourage him to enjoy books and stories, in the same way as my mother had encouraged me. I read him stories every night at bedtime, but also at other times. When we were in the car, he listened to audio books and followed the spoken word in the text. I searched bookshops and the local library for topics that would interest him. I also wrote stories for him in which he was the main character. When we went camping, I made up stories to tell him in the dark. We played lots of word games. I regret the day I taught him to play Scrabble – now that he is an adult, he beats me every time!

I also talked with my son. I talked *with* him and not *at* him. This was instinctive and based on my own childhood experiences, rather than on any professional training. It was only years later that I came across research that supports the importance of parent–child dialogue in relation to learning. I actively sought out ways to engage Gordon in discussions about what he was doing, got him to explain things to me and asked him open-ended questions that encouraged him to talk about what interested him. It is difficult to learn to read if you do not have an appropriate vocabulary – in Gordon's first year as my son, the widening of his vocabulary was astonishing.

Parents often notice things that teachers may not, which is understandable given that teachers have many children to monitor. As Gordon had no consistent adult carer until

I adopted him, no one had noticed that he was partially deaf. Within a few weeks, I became aware that he was not hearing well. I can only assume that staff thought his occasional lack of response was due to lack of intelligence or wilfulness. A hearing test determined that he had significant hearing loss in one ear due to glue ear. Gordon's own memory was of frequent earache in early childhood, and I suspect that he had had numerous untreated ear infections. It was at first suggested that some minor surgery would sort out the problem. However, once the specialist had a closer look, it was found that there was permanent damage to his middle ear. Gordon endured a number of painful operations to remove destroyed bone and tissue, but it was not possible to restore the hearing in that ear. Once the school was aware of the difficulty, they were able to make arrangements to ensure that Gordon could hear, and he also learned to speak up when he could not understand what was said.

Homework was a source of tension. The school day was tough for Gordon – it meant not only working hard at lessons, but at learning to cope with the unfamiliar social setting and managing his moods so that he could get by without drawing undue attention to himself. He came home as taut as a violin string after sitting still for most of the day, and desperately needed to unwind with play and physical activity outdoors. I tried to establish a routine for homework – should we do it at the end of the school day to get it over with so he could enjoy the rest of the evening? Should we wait until after the evening meal and risk him not being free to play when his friends called for him? Or should we save it till just before bedtime and risk disrupting the calm, happy atmosphere I tried to promote to help him settle to sleep? I was able to discuss some of these problems with Gordon's teachers. If they understood, they would turn a blind eye to his not completing homework. If they did not understand, I adopted a habit of completing the homework myself after he had gone to bed, writing with my left hand to make it it look more like his immature writing. I had no compunction about this – I knew if Gordon was to settle in school and at home, he needed not to be oppressed by homework, but to be free to learn outside school in a more informal way.

We spent a lot of time when Gordon was little at art galleries and museums. We lived close to Glasgow, which has a marvellous collection of free museums. He had an insatiable appetite for learning and a wide range of interests; his main interests in natural history and technology were well catered for during wet Saturday afternoons at the Kelvingrove Museum and the Museum of Transport. From one of his teachers, he also developed a love of history. I was always being surprised by the amount of knowledge he had acquired. One evening, when he was just twelve years old, we left a friend's twenty-first birthday party in Aberdeen at about 10pm and set off on the four hour drive home.

'You're going to have to talk to me, son, or I will go to sleep at the wheel.'

I wasn't serious, but Gordon took up the challenge immediately.

'Would you like to hear about King James IV?' he asked, 'I've been learning about him at school'.

'Sure,' I replied.

We reached Perth before he had run out of things to say about this Scottish king. I knew very little about King James IV myself, and was astonished when I checked the encyclopaedia the next day to find that Gordon's account had been entirely accurate.

I started to plan our family holidays around things that would further enhance Gordon's learning on topics that interested him. We walked along Hadrian's Wall and pretended we were Roman soldiers warding off the Celts. We visited Stirling, re-enacting ancient battles and working out troop movements from the vantage point of the Wallace Monument. We toured the capital cities of Edinburgh and London, soaking up the history. Gordon's interest in railways took us to York and later to North Wales to travel on the Ffestiniog Railway. I economised by using public transport, sharing cottages, camping and youth hostelling. We were fortunate that, as a teacher, I had the same long holidays as Gordon enjoyed, so there was plenty of time for these shared activities. None of the learning opportunities I provided for Gordon required special teaching skills or experience. The approaches I used could be employed by any caring parent. I don't believe that being a teacher made me a better parent, but I do know that being a parent made me a better teacher.

I often worried about how Gordon would cope once he left primary school. He would have to travel on the school bus to another town where the secondary school was large, and had a reputation for being rough. By chance, a few months before he transferred, I landed a temporary teaching post in the learning support department of this school and got to know the two teachers who worked there. These two women were to be incredibly supportive to Gordon throughout his time in the school. I also got to know the head teacher, Dr White, a wonderful man who seemed to know so many of the thousand pupils by name and had a genuine care for the most vulnerable among them. Knowing the school made me a lot less anxious, and when the time came for Gordon to start there, he settled well and thrived on the variety of subjects on offer, both within and beyond the curriculum. Dr White was interested in astronomy, and he frequently announced over the tannoy that there was to be something special in the night sky that evening. I have lost count of the number of nights I have been dragged by Gordon across a muddy field so we could see Jupiter or Venus or whatever planet was prominent at that point.

In his third year at secondary school, Gordon was excluded for three days for setting off the fire alarm. While staff checked whether this was a real fire or a false alarm, the whole school had to stand outside in the rain for twenty minutes. I received a call at work asking me to pick Gordon up; he was to be excluded from school for the next three days. At the time, I was working with young people in care, many of whom were also excluded from school. I knew all too well that if a young person is excluded once, they are much more likely to be excluded again. They tend to feel they have burned their boats so that there is no point in even trying to conform. Sometimes they gain status among their peers for being excluded, which encourages them to continue to flaunt the school's discipline. Or they may enjoy the taste of freedom exclusion from school brings, and manipulate situations so they can be excluded again. Returning to school after an exclusion means coping with the work you have missed, being told off for not completing your homework, and having teachers eye you askance, wondering when you are going to put the next foot wrong. So I felt sick as I drove to Gordon's school. How would I manage if he was continually excluded? What would the future hold for him if he could not finish his education at the local school?

When I arrived, I was taken to see Dr White, who was clearly reluctant to exclude the miscreant.

'Of all the young people in this school, Gordon is the last one I want to punish,' he explained to me. 'I really like the boy and I admire the way he has worked to overcome his difficulties. I don't want him to become a hero with the wrong crowd and, unfortunately, that is what is likely to happen if I exclude him, but I really don't have any choice – we had a thousand pupils standing out in the rain for twenty minutes this morning.'

At this point, Gordon was shown into the room, looking truculent and defiant. Dr White repeated to Gordon what he had just said to me. The tears welled up in Gordon's eyes. I was on the verge of tears myself: angry with Gordon and anxious as to how I was going to manage him at home for the next three days. I turned to look at Dr White and saw tears in his eyes too. That broke the ice with Gordon and the three of us were able to sit down and have a rational discussion about what had gone wrong and how to set it right. Gordon spent the next three days with our friend John, painting the exterior of his house. I wondered for a time if Gordon would see this as a real treat, a reward for misbehaviour, but the approach worked. Gordon felt he was paying something back for having caused everyone bother. Doing a good job with the painting raised his self-esteem, and spending the days with John calmed him down and put him in a much better frame of mind to return to school and knuckle down. He was never excluded again.

Dyslexia held Gordon back considerably at first, but once it was diagnosed, the school dealt with it expertly and he was able to make progress. Dyslexia may not only affect reading and writing, it may also affect short-term memory and the ability to organise information, making many simple tasks difficult. He found it hard to learn multiplication tables and number bonds. I had found this difficult myself as a child, but I had gradually found ways around the problem and could share my strategies with Gordon. His learning support teachers at secondary school were particularly skilled in this area and he gained confidence working with them. Nowadays he is thoroughly proficient on a computer, so writing is no longer the challenge it once was.

As well as the stimulus for learning within the home and from our circle of friends, Gordon learned a lot in the Scouts, the Junior Red Cross and in a drama club. Never one to sit around at home watching TV, he had a busy social life in the community and was an avid collector of badges and certificates. There was a thriving Bible class at our church, which he also enjoyed. We owe so much to the many dedicated volunteers who put their free time and talents into these activities.

Allowing Gordon the freedom to experiment at home was sometimes taxing, as some of his creative ideas led to glorious messes and disasters, but it was well worth giving him that freedom, as some of his ambitious plans had unexpected success. One of our friends was a telephone engineer, who was busy removing traditional dial phones and replacing them with touch-tone handsets. When Gordon spotted the old dial phones in the back of our friend's van, his creative brain went into overdrive. The house gradually filled up with disused handsets – grey, red and green. Some were turned into plant pots and other household items, but his most successful invention was the pair of speakers for another friend's car radio. These were much admired, and Gordon soon had orders for more. He had, and still has, a talent for recycling and repairing which has become invaluable as we have become more conscious of the environmental impact of our throw-away culture. One evening he came home, carrying a traditional oak dining chair. He placed it proudly by our second-hand table, which did not have a matching set of chairs. His find fitted exactly. 'If you like it, Mum, I can get you three more!' Of course, I was anxious to know where he had come by it, but once he had explained that he had found it in a skip and had already asked the owner if he could have it, I eagerly agreed. We had by this time moved to our larger house and I was still struggling to furnish it.

While Gordon was learning, I was learning too. When a ten-year-old boy is adopted, there is so much to learn at once. At the time, the days seemed long, but looking back, I now feel I had too little time with Gordon as a child. All too soon he was catapulted into adolescence and there was a whole new set of skills to be acquired. The change was all the more challenging because Gordon had to be treated as a much younger child in terms of attention, assurance, physical affection, playing and story reading – not so much because he was immature, but because he had had to grow up too quickly whilst caring for his younger siblings, and needed space to be a younger child again himself. The challenge as he became a teenager was to be able to give the affection and reassurance he craved, to a lanky, truculent adolescent who had reached the rebellious years.

It is often said that parenting is one of the hardest jobs, and one for which we receive no training. In my professional role, I have read most of what is written about parenting, worked my way through the manuals and programmes that are used in parenting education, and find myself saying over and over again, 'Yes, that is good advice, but it would not have worked with us.' Our situation was unique, and Gordon's needs were very special. No professional, however expert, could ever have developed the insights that I did into what Gordon needed and how to provide the best setting for him. Somehow, we got through, learning as we went.

I was lucky to be surrounded by friends and family who were supportive of me, gentle with any suggestions and, if they harboured critical thoughts about my parenting, wisely kept these to themselves. However, other people were overtly critical. There were those who thought that a single person should never adopt a child, and especially that a single woman should not be allowed to adopt a boy; they put Gordon's difficulties down to the lack of a male role model in the home. There were some people who thought I was too strict with Gordon, and others who thought I let him get away with far too much. A few thought that I was neglecting my duties if I left Gordon with family or friends for a weekend so that I could get a rest. Sometimes, it seemed as though I was blundering through a maze where every corner I turned led to a brick wall of criticism. And no one criticised me more than I criticised myself.

If Gordon was in difficulty at school or if there was trouble with a neighbour, I felt it reflected on me, not just as a parent, but as an adoptive parent. I did not believe I could be a real parent unless I was a really brilliant parent. Most of the time I tried too hard, exhausting myself with impossible demands, trying to be superhuman. It took a long time to accept that I only had to be a "good enough" parent.

I believe that adoptive parents of older children hold a trump card that birth parents do not have. Imagine the parents of a newborn child gazing lovingly at the tiny miracle they have just created. It is understandable if they have dreams of what their child will be and may do in the future. It is all too easy to burden children as they grow up with expectations to fulfil their parents' own unrealised ambitions. It must be difficult to avoid seeing the child as an extension of themselves. For an adoptive parent of an older child, there is less temptation to overburden the child with our dreams. Our children are already well developed with their own personalities and foibles; we realise they are ours for a very short time and our dreams are more likely to be simply that our children should be healthy and happy.

Truly, every day is a school day – there is always something fresh to learn. The further away I get from the period when I was bringing up my son, the more I realise that if I have any understanding about parenting, I picked most of it up as I muddled my way through those years. I also realise that the person I learned from most of all was Gordon.

8

Vodka and Irn-Bru

GORDON

When I left school, I started working on a farm. I loved that place. Every morning I started the day mucking out the barns. You might think shovelling muck is a horrible job, but for me it was just right. After that, there would be a whole variety of things needing to be done and there was so much to learn about farm machinery and how to take care of the stock of beef cattle and sheep. The farm family became a second family to me, and it wasn't long before they asked me to stay over during the week so I could be called on if there was a difficult calving during the night. It was perfect for me to be in the fresh air all day and then to come into the warmth of the farmhouse kitchen for a hot meal. When I was busy, things went well, but free time became tough to handle. I grew apart from the friends I had when I was younger and spent a lot of time on my own, drinking because it stopped me thinking about things that were troubling my mind.

When my time on the farm was done, I drifted a bit, doing lots of different jobs, but finding nothing permanent. When I was just nineteen, I met a Canadian woman and we married. A year later, we moved to Canada and I settled there.

JEANNIE

When Gordon left school, he enrolled in a youth training scheme at agricultural college and spent much of his time on placement at a local farm. The farm life was ideal for him. Working outdoors with animals in a predictable, secure environment helped him greatly. He got good reports from college and from the farmers supervising the placement. 'I've never seen a young person with such a natural way of handling stock!' one of the college tutors told me. 'I mean, I've never seen it before in a young person not raised on a farm.' Gordon was learning a lot and our teatable conversations were full of the gory details of helping out at obstructed births and castrating lambs. Much of the tension he had experienced at school seemed to disappear. But just as things began to get a whole lot better, they suddenly took a turn for the worse.

Anthea, our friendly young lodger, married and moved out and once again Gordon and I were on our own. Gordon was now seventeen, and apart from farmyard talk, had become as remote and uncommunicative at home as most teenagers. I was beginning to feel extremely weary from the effort of raising him by myself for the past seven years. I had so strongly felt the importance of repressing my own needs in order to be the best mum I could be for Gordon, that now I felt empty, tired and unsure of my own identity. I found there was little about life that I could enjoy, apart from work. So I poured myself into it, working longer hours and taking on a course of study that meant I was out more often.

At this stage, Gordon had a good friend, Richard. I knew the boy and his family well, and never had any concerns when Gordon left to go to Richard's house after our evening meal. He would often return about nine, saying he was tired and did not want anything to eat, and go straight to bed. He usually had an Irn-Bru bottle with him. Irn-Bru is a Scottish soft drink with a distinctly bright orange colour. It took me several weeks to realise that he had not been going to Richard's house at all, but that he was buying a bottle of Irn-Bru, tipping out most of the contents and filling it up with a mixture of Coke and vodka. The resulting mixture had the same colour as Irn-Bru and no discernable smell. Gordon was drinking himself to sleep almost every night.

I felt isolated from my friends who had children the same age as Gordon, because while they might be dealing with teenagers who drank one pint too many with their pals, or stayed out too late, they had no concept of caring for a young man who was drinking himself senseless on his own every night in an effort to self-medicate. Although I knew by this time that Gordon had mental health issues and I realised that he drank to ease his mental pain, I was powerless to stop the drinking or to help him see what he was doing. It was difficult to explain to others that I was not afraid of Gordon when he was drunk – at these times, he would be relaxed and affable. It was when the numbing effects of alcohol wore off that he became unpleasant and sometimes violent.

As time went on, he was less secretive about his drinking. I would get calls to collect him from the houses of friends or from dark corners of the town, where he had been found unconscious. In spite of the way he mistreated his body, he would always be up in the morning and off to work on the farm. He seemed oblivious to what his behaviour was doing to himself or to me. Desperately, I tried to patch up the things he broke around the house and to cover up in front of friends and neighbours. At some level, I knew it could not go on and that my failure to challenge his behaviour effectively was doing him no good, but I was paralysed, unable to take any action for fear the situation would become worse. No matter how bad it was, it was infinitely preferable to Gordon being incarcerated or my being forced to give him up. Inevitably, things eventually came to a head.

Gordon arrived home drunk in the early evening when Marie and John were visiting. They arranged for him to stay with them overnight until he sobered up. At two o'clock in the morning, he crept out of their house, walked a mile back to our home and, finding the door locked, climbed up on the porch roof, entered the house through the bathroom window and threatened to kill me. My shouts brought a neighbour running to my aid. Gordon tossed a bookcase full of books down the stairs, bursting open the wall of our downstairs toilet. He assaulted my neighbour, breaking his glasses. Someone called the police and Gordon was charged with breach of the peace. With the full support of my family and friends, I told him that he had now to leave home. I told him that although I would always be his mum and always love him and help him as best I could, I would not live with this level of violence any more. Gordon left and stayed for a short time at the farm.

Words cannot describe what an abject failure of a parent I felt. I blamed myself for being over-preoccupied with my work and studies. I blamed myself for being unable to find answers for his mental disorder. I blamed myself for not having acted sooner, for covering up the difficulties for too long. The new family we had tried to build together seemed to have been ripped apart.

Coming home from work on the day after Gordon had left the house, I found one of my neighbours had left a note asking for me to call in to see them. I hardly knew this couple. They had no children and kept themselves very much to themselves. Perhaps Gordon had done some damage to their property and they wanted to complain. I was surprised when the woman greeted me at the door with a warm smile. 'It's really my husband who wants to speak to you,' she said, 'but I just want to say first that I am so sorry for all the trouble you are having.' She showed me into their living room where her husband was waiting. They asked me to sit down and I sat nervously on the edge of my seat.

'I hope you don't think we are being nosy,' he began. 'But we live so near you that we couldn't help noticing what has been happening this last while. We have heard the shouts and we've seen Gordon coming home drunk. You might not know this, but it was us who called the police.'

'I am sorry you have been disturbed,' I replied defensively. 'Gordon moved out yesterday, so hopefully you won't hear any more noise.'

'That's what I wanted to talk to you about,' he went on. 'You've done the right thing.'

I stood up to go, mumbling again that I was sorry for their inconvenience. He urged me to stay as he had something more to say.

'I said I think you have done the right thing,' he insisted, 'But not because of us. You have done the right thing for Gordon. You probably don't know this, but I am a recovering alcoholic. I used to start drinking every Friday night and sober up just in time for work on Monday morning. Gradually I started not making it into work on Mondays. I spent so much of our money on booze, my wife had to borrow money to buy food and pay the mortgage. I lost my job and we nearly lost our home. I gave her a hell of a time.'

I turned to look at his wife. They were a straightforward, respectable couple with a beautiful home, a big car and all the trappings of a comfortable, middle-class life. His wife nodded and smiled. 'We don't talk about it much,' she said, 'but it is all true.'

Her husband went on. 'She used to beg me to stop drinking and I promised I would. Sometimes I managed for a week or two, but then I would go back to it. It had such a grip on me. Then one day she left me. It was the best thing she ever did. It brought me to my senses and I started going to the AA and haven't touched a drop since. That was ten years ago. I know I am still an alcoholic, and every day is a challenge. I could never have got this far if she hadn't done what she did.'

I thanked them for their help and stood up to leave.

'Don't go out there with your head hanging low,' he said as I left. 'We've watched you and your boy for years and we know you better than you think. That boy thinks the world of you and you have done a fine job of bringing him up. You are both going to get through this.'

On the night that Gordon was taken away, our dog, Susie, got out at some point during the mayhem, ran round to my parents' house and woke them by barking under their bedroom window. Realising something was not right, my dad dressed quickly and came round to help, arriving at the same time as the police. I was appalled that he had found out how bad things had become, as I had kept the worst from them. I was concerned that it would deeply upset them, but I ought to have known better. Both of them were more than able to cope with this most distressing side of Gordon's behaviour. It never affected their deep love for him, and they kept on reassuring me that things would improve. They were right. We not only got through it – it was a turning point.

Gordon is not an alcoholic. His abuse of drink was a sign of not being able to cope with the mental distress of his still undiagnosed condition. It would be some years before he got the professional help he needed, but from that night on, he had a new determination to find out about what was happening with his mind.

I managed to put down the deposit for a small flat for him in a nearby town and together we began to decorate it and find furniture. I continued to care for him as before, and it was easier to do so when he no longer lived at home, though he often came home for meals. He continued to need a great deal of support, especially as his work placement at the farm ended a few months later, and he was only able to get temporary jobs, some in the building trade and some as a care worker in homes for the elderly. The caring role suited him particularly well, but his first love was farming. The periods of unemployment hit him hard. Never one to sit about and feel sorry for himself, he got stuck into voluntary work, serving teas in a community café and working in a charity shop.

Just before his twentieth birthday, Gordon met and married a Canadian woman who was working in Scotland. Shortly after they married, they decided to move to Canada. When they told me of their plans, I was torn. It was so hard to let Gordon go, to be so unsure of how he would manage so far from his own family and culture and to know that I would not be able to continue to offer the regular support that I saw as essential. However, I was also keenly aware that the employment prospects in Scotland were poor, especially in farming. There seemed to be more opportunities for him in Canada. Above all, I respected his choices as an adult. I was amused and touched by how he had prepared for the conversation. In an effort to help him deal with the impetuous behaviour, which so often led him into trouble, I had taught him to sit down and consider situations, making lists of pros and cons. He came to me this time with a piece of paper with 'Reasons to move to Canada' on one side and 'Reasons not to move to Canada' on the other.

A couple of months later, I waved goodbye to them at the airport. My good friend Liz picked me up and took me out for the day – I think she was worried that I would be distraught. Naturally, I was sorry that it would be some time before I saw him again, but I had a strong sense that our relationship was as strong as ever, if not stronger. A phrase I had learnt as a child came back to me, 'Cast your bread upon the waters and you will find it again after many days.' I had done that most difficult of parenting tasks – I had let my child go – but I was confident that he would come back to me. That confidence is justified by the continuing strength of the bond between us seventeen years later.

9

The runaway train

GORDON

I had gone to see psychiatrists before and it had not been much of a success. I just could not connect with them. But one day in Canada I finally made an appointment that would change my life at last. I met a psychiatrist I could trust and to this day I call him my friend. Yes, you read right – I befriended my psychiatrist! I told him as well as I could what I was going through in my life and how my mind felt at times. He said to me, 'Young man, you have bipolar disorder.' He described in full detail what bipolar disorder is and something clicked in my mind. And I found out that there was help for me. I sensed a great wave of relief; at last I had a name for my problem in life. Bipolar was the name!

It was the beginning of another long journey to learn about this new part of me. And what a journey it was! At times it has brought me way too close to the edge, and sadly, at one time, it has nearly brought me to death's gates. Yet I have learned what this thing is and have learned so much about who I am in the process. The journey will not end till my time on this earth is done. I have not been alone in learning about bipolar disorder. Others have had to learn about it to help me in my times of need. I have been able to gather people around me who understand and with whom I can be myself. Sadly, in today's society there is a stigma attached to mental illness. People hear of a person having a brain disorder and think of a madman about to leap out and kill them. It is not that way for me. To me, it is just like having a heart problem or diabetes. It is just something that has to be managed and looked after.

Yes, it can be a curse many times over to be bipolar, and some days I wish I was not. Yet the blessing is this: I have become so aware of who I am; I know what will help me and what won't work for me. I have learned to avoid situations that will trigger my bipolar disorder and lead to great unhappiness for me and those around me. Many people are quite unaware of why they feel the way they do and don't truly understand who they are looking at in the mirror. Many people who are not bipolar could really benefit by having to sit down and look deep within themselves and take an inventory of what makes them tick.

If you care to know what it is like inside my mind, imagine a train driver in control of his engine. He's got a lot of things he has to keep his eye on – all the gauges in his cab, the signals and the condition of the track. He has to be alert and able to respond to whatever the morning throws at him. On an ordinary day, when I am well, that's what I'm like. I get up thinking about the tasks ahead, what I should wear, what I should eat for breakfast, what tools I will need to take with me for whatever job I am going to do that day. Then the phone rings. I listen and respond. Maybe it is someone saying I need to go somewhere on my way to work to pick up a piece of equipment. Maybe it is one of my kids telling me they are doing something special at school and asking me to please come and watch. I might go out to my vehicle and find it has a flat tyre. It's a bit annoying, but I can manage it – I just get my tools out and in a matter of minutes the spare is on. Maybe it is 30 degrees below and I have to spend a long time getting my vehicle started, but hey, I am a Canadian, that won't stop me! On an ordinary day, I am like the train driver, in charge of my mind, and I can manage whatever the day throws at me. I know I can reach the destination.

On the days when I am not so well, I am like a train driver with a runaway engine. I use up all my energy trying to get it back in control, but it is no good. If I get distracted, the train just goes faster. It tears down the track, bumping hard, throwing the passengers about, scaring folk. The signals flash past me, but I am unable to respond to them. I feel full of anger and despair: anger because it was not my choice to make this happen – I am stuck on a train with no brakes. Despair because I know that sooner or later there is going to be a crash. And after the crash, there is going to be hell to pay in putting things right with other people and sorting out the mess and picking myself up off the dirt again.

When I was younger, I had no idea how to stop the train. Now I have grown older, I know more about how my system works and how to find the brakes. I can predict when I get up in the morning that this is not going to be a good day. So sometimes I keep away from people until I feel better, or go for a long walk by myself to get my head round what is happening to me. Most folk who know me just let me be. They understand that I have bipolar and that is just how it affects me. They know that is the way I have to deal with it. It's not as frightening for me now I know what it is – my brain is just different from other people's brains.

Yes, I'm bipolar, but that is not all that I am, and with that in mind I have to work the same as everyone else to support myself, although I need employers to understand how my mind works. I often say that 'The messenger boy in my brain has gone to Mexico,' meaning that once in a while, I lose track of my thoughts and my mind wanders off. It takes a special kind of workplace and a special kind of boss to find ways to work around my disability and make use of my potential.

Where I work makes a big difference to me. Farm work is good for my mental health. I'm at my best when I am out in the fresh air and working with animals. Sadly, one of the side effects of my bipolar is that I tend to get scared of people and withdraw from them. Of course, this is just a trick of my mind that says, 'No one loves you and you are just a burden on the world'. But I don't feel like that around animals. I can tell them deep secrets and they don't tell those secrets to anyone. Animals respond well to me because I can be calm around them and I know what they need.

If I have a boss with a gentle manner and an understanding of who I am, I can be very productive and get lots of work done. I have a problem stopping once I get going on something, so my boss has to be strict with me and make sure that I have a break and rest. I have done many different farm jobs, but one of the best I have found is beekeeping. You might think that working with swarms of angry bees and getting stung would set off my bipolar, but it does the opposite. I'm forced to be calm and quiet and careful about how I move among the bees. People who own bee farms understand this. They tend to be calm themselves, and that makes them good bosses. This is perfect for me. It means things are explained slowly, so I can soak it all in and learn. Being bipolar doesn't mean I don't thirst for knowledge; in fact, my IQ is above average.

I started working on a bee farm for the first time last year, and my boss knew in a short time that I would work out as a beekeeper. Almost the first thing I did was get a book about beekeeping, and I did research on the internet. For the first few weeks amongst bees, I would wear my veil and would swat at anything that got near my face.

However, I was soon working without a veil and I started to love the little creatures. I learned to control my breathing – that is key to working with bees. Bee farming is always in the open, so I am outside all the time getting fresh air.

I know I can't work in a high-powered kind of job where there is a lot of information coming fast and quick choices to be made. My psychiatrist tells me I have far too good a brain to be working on a farm and I should go to college and get a better job, but right now, that's not for me. I have trouble doing more than one or two tasks at a time – if I try to do more than that, I get confused and frustrated and that sets off my bipolar. Once I have a clear understanding of what my task is, I can organise my work in my mind. Then the job gets done and you would never know I had a mental illness. In fact, you would probably want to hire me!

JEANNIE

One Saturday morning, while Gordon was still working and living at the farm, he returned home after a night shift. He was clearly unwell – pale, trembling and uncommunicative. He lay on the sofa, hunched in the foetal position and staring wildly about him. For a time I simply observed him, hoping he would improve, but after an hour he showed no change, except that he kept muttering to himself. He did not appear to have a temperature, but I called our family doctor anyway. He suggested that Gordon was having an acute attack of his undiagnosed psychiatric condition. He wanted to have Gordon admitted, but Gordon was adamant that he did not want to go to hospital. However, he agreed to take some medication. Within a short time, he visibly relaxed and was able to tell us that he could no longer cope with the clamour of voices in his head. It was the first time he had told me that he heard voices.

For some weeks, Gordon continued on the medication and attended sessions with a community psychiatric nurse.

The nurse explained to us that in Gordon's brain, it sometimes seemed as though twenty conversations were going on at once, and that he could not filter out the ones that he should ignore or postpone. The resulting "noise" made him anxious and unable to respond appropriately to things and people around him. Although this analogy was helpful, the only solution that the nurse could offer to dampen the noise was more medication. As Gordon's symptoms disappeared, we ceased to attend the sessions. Gordon stopped taking the medication and I did not insist he continue, as I was shocked by how lethargic the pills made him. They slowed him down so much that he could not do his beloved work on the farm, and they dampened down his emotions to the extent that he seemed like a zombie, with no personality and unable to reason constructively about his condition.

From this point on, both of us accepted that he was suffering from an unspecified mental illness. Neither of us was keen to investigate it further, although I was concerned that Gordon should learn to manage the effects. He seemed to be able to do so, most of the time. Part of the recovery lay in consistency, avoiding situations that made him anxious and using visual and cognitive means of communicating his experiences. On one occasion, when I had spent some time with him talking of how he might respond when he felt there was too much "noise", he said, 'Thank goodness you understand, Mum. I don't think there is anyone else who does. I am not sure I understand it myself.'

Part of that understanding meant allowing Gordon a great deal of space, both physical and emotional. It meant accepting that there were times when he had to be on his own, and times when only physical activity could help him silence the "noise" in his brain. In social situations, this could cause difficulty and embarrassment, but Gordon was so universally liked that people who knew him well simply accepted his sudden striding out of a room, or being unable to join in a group activity.

Years later, after a period of illness in Canada, Gordon began to see a psychiatrist whom he trusted. Finally, he felt he had a label to put on the condition that haunted him. The diagnosis was bipolar disorder, which at first provided intense relief. We were finally able to give the condition a name to family and friends, were able to recommend reading on the subject and we believed that, provided Gordon took the appropriate medications, all would be well.

For Gordon, a long journey began of coming to terms with his situation and of working with his psychiatrist to find how best to treat it. I knew little of the condition, so started to learn about bipolar disorder and the types of medication that are normally prescribed. His psychiatrist had suggested that Gordon would benefit from a support network: a small group of people with whom Gordon would agree to share some of his clinical history and who might be able to encourage him to take his medication. Gordon wanted me to be part of this group, even though he was living four thousand miles away, so I tried to encourage him to stick with his medication, even when it seemed unnecessary. I urged him not to miss his psychiatric appointments. As far as I knew, Gordon mostly complied, but there were periods when he felt the pills were having unpleasant side effects and stopped taking them. He also told me that he hated the "flat" feeling he had when on the medication. I worried about that, and about the whole issue of labelling.

It concerned me that it was possible to concentrate on treating a categorised illness, instead of responding to the needs of an individual, especially one like Gordon, who had such a complex history. Earlier in my life, I had been influenced by some of the writing of R.D. Laing, the Scottish psychiatrist who did much to challenge the medical model of mental illness. I therefore wanted to listen to

Gordon attentively and to understand what he might be trying to communicate to us and to himself through his illness. However, these concerns were overridden by my fear that, without his medication, Gordon might severely injure himself, be imprisoned or even kill himself. Finally, what persuaded me to encourage Gordon to keep going with his prescribed treatment was that he himself found the diagnosis of bipolar disorder helpful, and had a lot of trust in his psychiatrist, who not only offered him prescription medications, but also regular consultations, cognitive therapy and advice about diet and light therapy.

Bipolar disorder was previously known as manic depression and at its simplest is described as suffering from episodes of very low moods (depression) and periods of high energy and excitement (mania). The condition has complex definitions and many different forms – the International Statistical Classification of Diseases and Related Health Problems recognises at least twelve variations. It has been suggested that we all exist somewhere on a bipolar spectrum. Gordon was diagnosed with Bipolar Disorder Type II, indicating someone who has had manic episodes but is more likely to be depressed. There are many theories about what causes bipolar disorder. Most agree that there is a hereditary connection, but it is also believed that without a trigger such as trauma in childhood, the inherited predisposition will not necessarily lead to bipolar disorder developing. Recent studies using brain scanning techniques suggest brain chemistry may play an important role in the condition.

Awareness of the medical basis of his illness made Gordon's more bizarre actions, which could so easily be seen as reckless and selfish, more understandable. An event which took place shortly after he emigrated to Canada illustrates this. He was seen driving his car erratically and at high speed on the highway and was reported to the Royal Canadian Mounted Police. A patrol car followed him and over the megaphone they ordered him to stop, but Gordon simply increased his speed. Another patrol car was summoned and Gordon was forced to a halt between the two vehicles. He was hauled out of his car and spread-eagled on the bonnet while the officers searched him for a weapon. There is no doubt such police action was necessary – Gordon was being a risk to himself and to other road users. But Gordon was not thrill seeking, nor was he involved in any criminal activity. He was also sensible enough to know he could not evade the police. He told me later he believed at the time that he was fleeing from a hallucination that was terrifying him. When the police car pursued him, it became part of the nightmare. Fortunately, on this occasion the officers recognised that there were mental health issues. They therefore did not charge him, but escorted him to the hospital, where he was offered treatment.

Gordon's behaviour has since been under much better control and he has not had a major manic episode for many years. Being able to identify his difficulty, to explain it to others and to receive understanding have all greatly reduced the stress that can trigger a manic attack. Avoidance of undue stress and eating a healthy diet supplemented by vitamins and regular checkups all contribute to effective self-management of his illness.

When Gordon's marriage broke up, I was fearful that he would become seriously ill again. As well as dealing with the painful business of separation and divorce, he was isolated from his Scottish family, homeless and in financial difficulties. However, my fears were groundless. Gordon has always been someone who is able to call on resources deep within him, which is surprising, considering how fragile a person he can sometimes appear to be. There were certainly some setbacks, but Gordon has gradually built up his resilience and renewed his determination to manage his illness.

'People think that because I am bipolar, that is all I am,' he told me, shortly after he set up house on his own. 'But I am going to show them there is more to me than bipolar.'

By now, I was also a lot more familiar with my own mental health status – I had been a bit depressed from time to time in my life, but during the summer of 1997, when Gordon was already settled in Canada, I experienced a long and much more severe period of low mood, and for the first time I was medicated and unable to work for several weeks. The low mood was not a reaction to my circumstances: I had recently met the lovely man who was to become my husband, Gordon was safe and I was doing very well in my career and had a full social life. We had just had a great walking holiday in the mountains of Spain and I was happy to be going back to work, when suddenly I crashed. I lost all confidence in my ability to do anything, found I could take no pleasure in any of my normal activities, had nothing to say to people and hardly had the energy to get up and get washed in the morning. Reluctantly, I agreed to take medication, as I began to be frightened of the way I was feeling and the odd sensations I was experiencing. Within a few weeks of taking the drugs, I was much better and able to return to work, although it was almost a year before I really felt well again. I know the experience was nothing like Gordon's, but it deepened my empathy with him.

One of the positive outcomes of being forced into acknowledging how ill I had become was that I now understood my own mother better. It is possible that she suffered from untreated depression for a great part of her life. She was a very loving, caring woman, but I had found it all too easy to be critical of her and to remember only the times I felt rejected. When I was a teenager, she was in her fifties, had raised seven children and had the long-term care of my disabled sister. It is not surprising that she rarely had the energy for me!

One in four people will experience a mental health problem at some point in their lives, yet the stigma is so great that many fear to talk about it with friends and colleagues. Gordon has always been very open about his condition and now finds that even employers are unfazed by it, as he has a good reputation as a worker in his local community. Each time I have visited him in Canada or he has visited us in Scotland, I have found him more stable, more optimistic and much more able to manage his moods. Two years ago, while on a trip to Vancouver with him and his children, he took a walk with me one evening, and confided in me that with the full approval of his psychiatrist, he had stopped taking his medication. He was concerned that I would disapprove, but during the two weeks that we had spent together I had noted that his mood was stable and his cognitive functioning had improved, so I could not reasonably object. I was impressed with the amount of insight he now had into his condition. He has learned that for him, stress can lead to unbearable levels of anxiety, which can trigger an attack, so he is developing ways of avoiding undue stress in his life. He also recognises that he needs a proper rhythm of rest and work and a good diet. Most of all, he has helped other people to understand why he needs to be on his own at times. I think this is why the prairie lifestyle in Canada has been so important to him. He loves the endless open spaces where the population is sparse, the highways empty and the sky vast and astonishingly beautiful: bright blue by day and velvety dark at night. I have often taken a stroll with him when the sky is lit by stars more brilliant than are normally seen in our light-polluted corner of Scotland. I have been there several times when the heavens become incandescent with the shimmering, iridescent curtains of the Northern Lights and I can understand why he loves it and feels at peace there.

I am dealing with my own depressive illness much better too. There is something so empowering in realising that you can, at least most of the time, self-manage your illness. For me, the first step was acceptance. I recognised that although I did not have a full-blown case of illness until late on in life, I had been depressed on and off since my family moved to Aberdeen when I was eight years old. I also accepted that there is a strong likelihood that I could get depressed again. The next step was to begin to recognise the warning signs – for me, it is a heightened sense of anxiety that leads to feelings of failure and inability to carry on. I am now more open with people – for most of my life I had not told even those who were very close to me that I was ill. It seemed like a sign of weakness, as if I was pleading for special treatment. Since I have shared more widely how ill I have been, I have been enormously encouraged by how often others have opened up and shared with me their pain, either because they too have mental illness, or because someone they love also suffers. While medication was necessary for me at one point, I hope never to need it again, due to my improved self-management. I have found two things particularly helpful to my recovery – person-centred counselling and a form of meditation called mindfulness. The counselling has helped me understand and come to terms with some of the painful things that happened to me as a child, and the meditation has helped me find practical means of dealing with stress and detaching myself from worrying over the past and fearing the future, so that I can concentrate on living in the present.

I wondered whether to mention my depressive illness in this book. Would readers think that perhaps I ought to have been vetted more thoroughly and not allowed to adopt a child? Would they imagine that some of the difficulties my son experienced could be blamed on me? Or would the stigma of mental illness put them off the story completely? In the end, I decided to be honest, partly because I believe strongly that we need to lift the veil on mental illness and reduce the fear that still surrounds it. There are many people who have at times been mentally ill who are also competent parents, caring individuals and successful in their careers. Mental ill health should not exclude us from taking our full part in life where we can.

In the end, I wanted to write about my depressive illness because I think it is central to the story of my adoption of Gordon. Suffering from occasional bouts of depression makes me who I am; it gives me enormous capacity for understanding others, it makes me less judgemental and more empathetic than I might otherwise have been. It gave me the depth of character I needed to deal with the darkest parts of being Gordon's parent.

GORDON

These words from my mum have given me more courage to go on, knowing how we have both recovered from illness. Growing up with my mum, I could see she was human – not a Super-Mum! There are times, as I grow older, when I am there for her in the way she has always been there for me.

10

As if one mum was not enough

GORDON

One of the many things I love about my mum is that she has an open mind about my birth family. She always said to me, 'When the time comes and you are ready for it, I will help you and support you in finding your birth family.' This made me trust her more than ever and it helped me in times when I would be walking down a crowded street and I would wonder, 'Am I related to any of these people?' I often looked in the mirror and wondered who I looked like. I knew I looked like no one in my new family and I came to be at peace with that. My adopted mum's family surrounded me with such love and acceptance that it didn't matter that I was different. Later in life, I came to think of myself as blessed to have such a large family and it is kind of fun to watch people try to figure out who's who! Yet in my mind it is straightforward and not complicated at all. If you are not an adopted person yourself, then all you can have is a slight understanding of the complex web of people an adopted person calls family.

Before I left Scotland for Canada, I signed up with an adoption register so that any of my birth family could find me if they wanted to contact me. My birth family had been split up when I was taken into care and no one knew where they all were.

Where I now live in Canada is seven hours behind UK time, so I was sound asleep when the phone rang. At first, I could not take in what was happening and then I heard a voice that kindled some kind of distant memory. The cheery voice was saying, 'Hello, Gordon, I'm your mum!' I felt the tears run down my face and part of me was upset that there were so many miles between me and that voice. I could not reach out at that moment and give my birth mum a hug and tell her how much I had wanted to hear her voice and to meet her. It was like no time had passed at all. I told her quickly about being adopted and how my adoptive mum agreed with me contacting my birth family. She said to thank my adoptive mum for doing such a fine job of raising me. We just connected and the conversation flowed with ease. I tried to keep the racing thoughts and questions in my mind from pouring out. I had waited so long and had so many questions to ask. I found out she was married again and living in Morecambe. After much talking, I finally said goodbye. But sleep was not going to come to me now.

One part of me was on cloud nine. Finally, there were answers to my many questions and yet there was deep fear as well. What if this all backfires? What if my mum had not meant that she would support me in finding my birth mum, but had just said it to keep me happy? I had to get on top of these rapid thoughts that would not leave me in peace. It was time to pick up the phone and see just how strong my relationship was with my mum and just how truly she was behind me in meeting my birth family. I was many miles away and so I decided to ask my adoptive mum to meet up with my birth mum. Then these questions kept coming to my mind. How would this change my world? How would I be able to fit two mums into my life? How could I love both of them and not make either one feel as though they were being left out? I was on my own with my problem and there was no one to ask how they did it. I would have to reach deep inside myself and find courage and take the consequences, good or bad.

Ignoring how scared I felt, I picked up the phone and called my mum in Scotland. She was pleased I had found my birth mum and was right behind my plan that the two of them should meet, but I was still afraid. What if these two women didn't get along with each other? What if they couldn't find a way to share me, and worried that I might spend more time with the other? How was I going to play this hand?

I was absolutely certain of my mum's place in my life. She was the one who had raised me and put up with all sorts of stuff and always stuck by me, even when my behaviour was way out of line. Yet there were still questions burning me up. Where did I come from? Who do I look like? What is my true family history? My mum had never had to deal with these nagging questions, but she showed her love for me by being willing to meet with my birth mother and to begin to find answers for me.

I tried all that day to think of other things and yet all I had in my mind was how I could fit these two worlds together. I had heard stories where things had gone really wrong with adopted people finding their birth families. Eventually, remembering how well the two phone conversations had gone, I decided to relax and take one step at a time.

The meeting between my two mums was planned, and that meeting would change the course of my life for the good. It would bring me even closer to my adoptive mum and give me a deeper love and respect for what she had done for me. More importantly, it was a meeting that would finally answer my big question: 'Who am I?'

JEANNIE

When Gordon called me and asked if I would meet Kathleen, his birth mother, I accepted the challenge without hesitation. For two years I had tried to find her on his behalf. The social work department provided me with an address, but it was out of date. I contacted the priest of the parish the family had once lived in, but although he was understanding, he was unable to help. I wasn't sure where else to turn. I knew that Gordon had left his name on an adoption contact register, but for a long time, nothing had come of that. Although I was persuaded that Gordon had the right to contact his birth mother and I was therefore committed to helping him find her, I was concerned that he might be disappointed when he did.

I sometimes found that other people did not understand how I could be so positive about this woman I had never met, but I found no difficulty in appreciating how deeply a woman may love her child without having the capacity to nurture him appropriately. I often doubted my own capacity, and was concerned at how limited my personal resources sometimes felt. Yet I had everything on my side that Gordon's birth mother had not had: a safe, comfortable home; financial security; a career I enjoyed; a warm, loving extended family; and a supportive community. I wondered how well I would have coped if things had been different.

I now felt that Gordon being in contact with his birth mother posed no threat to our relationship. We had bonded very securely and I had no apprehension that loving his birth mother would mean he had any less love for me. We had been through some very testing times together which would have fractured a less secure mother and son bond. I had no doubts about the importance of my place in his life, nor had I any doubts that his birth mother also had a place, and that both she and Gordon deserved to know one another. So I was delighted he had found her and, although anxious in case he got hurt, I was keen to do anything I could to make their reunion a success.

Driving south to Morecambe, I reflected that not only was I at ease with meeting the woman who had given birth to Gordon, I was also intrigued! From the first day I had met him, I had loved Gordon's quirky character, his affectionate nature and his warm and open personality. Although our life together had formed much of who he was, I knew that he must have both inherited characteristics from his birth family and also absorbed traits from them in those early years. I wondered if I would recognise Gordon in Kathleen. I thought of stories to tell her about what Gordon had done in the years she had missed. It was not hard to think of amusing things to illustrate his madcap, adventurous spirit and his highly imaginative, wacky schemes. One of his favourite activities in his early years was burying precious toys to hide them from some unknown danger. Toys from the Star Wars movies were popular at the time, and Gordon especially loved his Yoda, a tiny plastic figure with a wise and inscrutable smile. Yoda would be buried in the garden, at the beach and, on one memorable occasion, behind the dashboard of the car. All would go well until the time came for Yoda to be resurrected. Then the garden would be dug over from end to end, or I would find Gordon, armed with a screwdriver, tearing off the dashboard in an effort to recover his tiny companion.

Before I left home that morning, I had gathered some photographs of Gordon to give to Kathleen. I felt so rich compared to her in having so many happy memories of his childhood and youth. I wanted to share these with her and do what I could to make up for the lost years. Rummaging around to find the photographs, I came across a little wooden car that I had kept since Gordon was ten. I recalled the occasion when I found him in the garage, hacking away at a piece of driftwood and some dowel rod. Patiently, he constructed a little wooden car with wheels made from the dowel. I was delighted he had done so well, but Gordon was disappointed, as the wheels did not turn as freely as he wished. Later, there were much more advanced models, but this one meant a lot to me, and I had kept it. I used to joke I would show it to people at his twenty-first birthday party and he would reply, 'Don't you dare!' I popped the little car into the bag with the photos, meaning to share the story with Kathleen, and to leave the car with her if she would accept it.

Kathleen and I had agreed to meet on the promenade in Morecambe. As I approached the spot, I felt physically sick with anxiety. To add to all my other worries, I had no idea if we would recognise each other – we had not exchanged photographs or told each other what we would be wearing. Then, among the seaside crowd, I suddenly spotted a small woman who was looking directly at me with a smile so like Gordon's that it was like seeing an old friend.

'Oh, you are so like Gordon!' I cried out.

She kept on smiling. 'And you are just like Gordon told me!' she answered. Without any hesitation we hugged and any last feeling of awkwardness vanished.

We spent the day together, first having coffee in a café, walking on the prom and finally Kathleen insisted on taking me for a meal.

'A sandwich will be fine,' I protested, but she had her heart set on something else.

'No, I have been saving up for this,' she said. 'I am going to take you to a restaurant for a proper sit-down meal!'

There was so much to talk about that the day flew past. I told her stories of what Gordon had got up to as a small boy and of how he had grown up to be the sort of young man both of us could be proud of. She told me stories of his childhood I had not heard before. They fitted exactly with what I already knew of his personality – it felt like finding the final piece of a jigsaw puzzle.

Although I had been told in detail the reasons for Gordon and his siblings being taken into care, it was helpful to have Kathleen's perspective on it and to find that she had no animosity towards the authorities for taking the action they did. 'I couldn't look after him – he had a better life with you,' she said. I could not find it within myself to have anything other than compassion for a woman who had given birth to six children and yet had been unable to bring up any of them due to her own difficulties and the violence in her home.

Kathleen was also able to tell me much more about her extended family. I knew from the social workers and from Gordon the important role Kathleen's parents and her brother had played in protecting the children and helping to bring them up, but I now had a much stronger sense of what this family was like and the difficulties they had had to overcome. Gordon had often told me of his Uncle Jim (Kathleen's brother) and how much he loved him. Jim was now giving Kathleen a lot of support and was a key figure in her life.

Later, I drove Kathleen back to her home on the outskirts of the town. She made me a cup of tea and I gave her the photographs and the little wooden car Gordon had made. 'This is a little bit of his childhood I would like you to have,' I said. She was very moved by the gift and rushed over to her display cabinet and took down a small, plastic racing car with the number six marked on the side of it. This was the decoration on the cake she had bought for Gordon's sixth birthday. I was speechless. Gordon had been taken into care just before his sixth birthday, and Kathleen had not seen him since. Yet she had bought him a birthday cake in the hope she would see him on his birthday, and had saved this memento for over twenty years. She insisted I take the car. I protested long and hard as I knew how much it had meant to her, but she won the argument. I treasured the little car and gave it to Gordon on my next visit to Canada. It now sits on a shelf in his house, among his most precious possessions.

Before I left that day, we asked a neighbour to take our photograph together. Gordon has that photograph in his home in Canada and often says it is his favourite – his two mums together, hugging and smiling. Visitors ask him who the people are, and he enjoys seeing their surprise when he tells them the story.

The drive home seemed to last forever – I was emotionally exhausted and desperate to get back so I could call Gordon and tell him about the day. He was thrilled with my account of the meeting and had already spoken with Kathleen.

A few weeks later, we started planning for Gordon and his family to come home the following year so that he could meet up with Kathleen. By this time, she had moved from Morecambe and it was arranged that we would meet her and Gordon's Uncle Jim in a motorway café on the M74, to avoid either party having to travel too far. We were all feeling extremely excited and nervous as the time for the meeting came near. We had just started our journey when I got a call on my mobile from Jim.

'We can't come,' he said. 'I'm terribly sorry, but Kathleen can't make it. She is so nervous – she has worked herself up into a state and doesn't think she can go through with it.'

I asked if I could speak to Kathleen. It was some moments before she came to the phone.

'I know you are nervous of meeting him,' I began, 'and he is a bit nervous too. But really, there is no need. You and I get on fine. You will find it easy to get on with Gordon too.'

'But it's all the stuff in the past,' she said.

I assured her Gordon had put that behind him. 'Please come! He has come such a long way to meet with you. You will be so sad if you don't try, and so will he.'

Finally she agreed, and they set off. I drove to the service station where we were to meet, terrified that there would be a further delay. We arrived in good time. Gordon paced up and down, looking out of the window and going to the door every few moments to check out each car that entered the car park. I wondered if he would recognise Kathleen and Jim when he saw them, but there was no doubt of that. He shot forward to greet them as they drove in and was immediately engulfed in hugs and kisses. We left them on their own for a while. When they came into the restaurant, we all had a meal together and there was furious catching up with news and getting to know one another.

'I wondered what this would be like,' said Jim. 'One guy, two mums – I was scared you might be tearing each other's hair out!'

Kathleen and I looked at each other and laughed. The idea that there should be any animosity between us seemed absurd after our first meeting. Kathleen accepted my role with her son, just as I accepted hers. Our relationship has remained positive. We don't see each other often but we sometimes talk on the phone and we have met up whenever Gordon and his children have visited the UK. Even if she lived closer, I doubt if we would meet much more. We live quite different lives and have nothing whatsoever in common – except sharing a son, which creates a strong bond between us. Recently, I celebrated my sixtieth birthday and was delighted to receive a card from Kathleen. I was moved by the message she had written inside: 'From Mum Kath to Mum Jeannie, thank you for everything you have done for me'.

Sadly, Gordon's Uncle Jim died a few years ago. As Gordon was unable to travel from Canada to attend the funeral, my husband and I went to represent him. There, we met more of the extended birth family and enjoyed the same warm welcome I had had from Kathleen the first time I met her. Sad as the event was, it was a real pleasure to be able to talk about Gordon with uncles and cousins who remembered him. One of the most remarkable things about the experience was the way in which Kathleen showed no embarrassment; she took pride in introducing us as 'Gordon's other mum and dad', and telling her relatives that I had brought him up.

I understand what Gordon meant when he asked before he met Kathleen, 'Who am I?' My parents both died some time ago, but I often hear their voices in what I say, and see them in the things I do. I am not always pleased by that – sometimes I find myself "being just like my mum" in a way I dislike! However, there is something in the continuity of identity that is affirming and reassuring.

When I tell the story of how I met Kathleen, some people seem to regard me as a kind of hero, which I find quite absurd. It was certainly an unusual sort of experience, but a helpful one for me. Knowing his birth mother has brought me even closer to Gordon and having her blessing helps tie up some of the loose threads for me and, I suspect, for her. Most of all, knowing that we get on so well together has helped Gordon piece together his shattered early life.

11

An even bigger family

GORDON

The day I first held my son in my arms, I got a sense of what my birth mum must have felt the day she first held me and how my adopted mum must have felt the day that she took me into her world to be her son.

Yes, I had found my birth family and I had my adopted family as well, but this child was truly my family. Part of me was scared stiff and part of me was thrilled. I was humbled by this small person in my arms. He needed me in every way and was helpless to do anything for himself. As I held my son, I spoke to him and he seemed to know who I was, and the bond was instant between us.

Later, a daughter came into my world and I was again in sheer awe at the beauty of a new, helpless human life. I held her in much the same way as I had held my son, and there was the same thrilling instant bond between us.

I love my kids to bits and see so much of myself in them. I see both what I like and what I dislike about myself and, of course, as they grow older, I can see their own characters develop as well. I am so grateful that by the time they were born, I had a good idea of who I was as a person, and felt connected to both my birth family and my adoptive family. I'm a lucky man to have my mum and my birth mother "on the same page" and for them both to enjoy their grandchildren. My mum is as much their granny as my birth mother is, and for me this is great to see. Even in "normal" families, there is often strife between grandparents. There is nothing like that in my family. My children have three sets of grandparents: my mum and dad, my birth mum and my in-laws. All of them work well together and want only what is best for my children. I could not dare ask for anything better and it is a blessing for my kids to see the harmony among their grandparents.

I had grown up and emigrated to Canada before my mum met and fell in love with Ted. It took a bit of getting used to at first. I had four marvellous uncles that were like fathers to me, especially my Uncle David. My mum had lots of men friends too, so there were enough guys around to take the place of a father. My mum had always seemed strong and happy on her own, so at first I was a bit put off by the whole thing, and suspicious of this man who was dating my mum. Would he be kind to her? How would he feel about me? It didn't take long before I knew for sure he was worthy of my mum. He's a quiet, steady man with a very laid-back attitude, and a wicked sense of humour. I soon found him to be someone I could love and accept and fit into my world with ease. I guess once I chose to be part of the Mackenzie family, it became easier to let other people in. My experience with the Mackenzie family taught me that blood is not really thicker than water – it is the quality of the relationship that counts, not the genes.

The night before their wedding, Ted drove me back to the cottage where we were staying. During the drive, I was quiet, because I was trying to summon up the courage to ask him if I could call him "Dad". I wasn't a child any more – indeed, I was married and a father myself – but this step was important to me. I felt it would make fitting him into my world a whole lot easier if I could call him Dad. I was sitting in the car with him and my mind played over and over what to say, until I blurted it out: 'Can I call you Dad?' To my great relief, he did not hesitate for a second, but quietly and firmly said, 'Yes, I would be so pleased if you would call me Dad'. I could have sailed to the moon at that moment without a rocket! My heart was shouting for joy and the sense of relief that washed over me was like a great warm and peaceful tidal wave. My new dad is someone who completes my family for me. I can talk to him about anything and have fun with him as well. Most importantly, he is there for me, just like my mum. He has a daughter and a son, so all at once I gained a new step-brother and sister and more nieces and nephews.

JEANNIE

When I was thirty-two and adopted Gordon, I could not have imagined that I would be part of the large, blended family I belong to today. I met Ted when I was forty-five and together we have three children and five grandchildren. It takes some explanation, especially as Ted is an adoptive parent too. I never expected to meet a life partner, far less to get married. When Gordon was young, I didn't date – I had neither the inclination nor the energy, which is just as well as Gordon really needed me all to himself at that point. When he got older, I went on a few dates, which led nowhere. I was completely open with Gordon about the men I saw and he enjoyed vetting them, but was sceptical about any of them being right for me, telling me I needed someone really special. I agreed, but there didn't appear to be anyone like that available. Most men seemed to find me far too self-reliant and independent. So I accepted that I would continue to be single and, by and large, I was happy with that. Friends would try to introduce me to prospective partners and despair of how fussy I was. My reply was that I had only three criteria. In the first place, he had to be the sort of man who would allow me to be myself and not try to mould me into some stay-at-home, sweet little housewife. Secondly, he had to share my values. Thirdly, he had to be able to make me laugh. As I am tall for a woman, I would also add that it would help if he was taller than me and I did not have to look down on his bald patch! My friends gave up hope, telling me I was looking for the impossible. I had to agree with them, and I secretly suspected that I set the bar so high partly because I was happy on my own.

When Ted turned up, he not only more than met all the criteria, but also had a thick crop of curly hair, so no bald patch (although I would have to stand on a chair to be sure!). We have been unbelievably happy together. We both care deeply about families and communities that struggle with poverty, ill health and lack of opportunity. In different ways, we have spent our working lives fighting inequalities. It is not all serious, though; as Gordon says, he has a wicked sense of humour that appeals to me and we spend much of our time in laughter. Above all, he is a deeply caring person and not the least part of our happiness is that we share our children and grandchildren, joining in the good times and supporting them through the hard patches.

When I set out to adopt, I did not think ahead to grandchildren; trying to imagine that one day my son would be grown up was hard enough. When Gordon called me from Canada and asked me if I felt I was old enough to be a grandmother, I was thrilled to hear there was a new member of the family on the way. I have since been closely involved with both children, in spite of the distance. We often talk on the phone and I write them both letters every week, starting with little picture books when they were young, graduating to puzzles and crosswords and, finally, to proper letters. They have spent a number of holidays with us both here and in Canada.

One of the activities they enjoy very much when we are together is hearing stories of what their father did when he was little. I make these as light and amusing as I can, but as they grow older, they want to know why he was taken from his birth family and why I decided to adopt him. We answer these questions simply, trying to take into account what they are able to understand, and shielding them from the darker side of things for the moment. I have made them a little booklet with their complex family tree. The oldest one has met several members of the birth family and has a good understanding of the situation. Both children seem to accept readily that Daddy has a mental illness and is sometimes not well enough to come and see them.

Following the breakdown of Gordon's marriage four years ago, the children live with their mother and her new partner and Gordon lives nearby. There is no doubt that he finds contact with the children as a single parent not at all easy. Caring for young children on your own is demanding for anyone, but Gordon has to cope with continual "noise" in his brain. When there is another adult around, he can take a break until he is able to cope, but that option is not open to him when he has the children on his own. Dealing with more than one piece of incoming information can be hard enough for him, but the normal noise of children playing, their demands for attention and bickering with one another can mean he quickly reaches overload. Having them round for a meal or to stay overnight is therefore hard for him, so he tends to take them to the park, or drives them to a friend's house where he can have some help. The best times are when he is with us – with our support, he can relax and spend quality time with the children, taking the older one out for something they call "guy time", tucking the little one into bed and reading her stories. He can be a wonderful parent, full of fun and mischief, gentle but firm and affectionate with both children.

I think Gordon would love to find a partner who would

not only understand his condition, but also see beyond it to the quality of person he is. He feels he could then be a more involved dad to his two children. He is much stronger mentally than he was when he first married, and much more able now to build a strong relationship. He complains that he can't find anyone, but I remind him that I did not meet my soul mate until I was forty-five, so he has time!

12

Siblings

GORDON

In a perfect world, I am sure no one would ever want to be adopted. We all have a dream of the perfect family unit, where everyone gets on with each other most of the time and there is no pain, but sadly human nature is flawed and that is not always possible.

Now I can look back at my past and feel hardly any of the pain from the troubles in my early family life. But it has taken a lot of grit and tears to get here. Sometimes it has been down to me to be first to forgive. I have found peace through being willing to shrug things off and make the first move.

I found my younger birth siblings again and we have had wonderful times of reunion, but they were not at the same place in life, and did not want anything to do with our birth mother. I found this painful, but I realise that being older, I understood more about why things happened in the way they did, and I could forgive her more easily. They know I am in contact with our birth mother, but I have to walk a fine line, not letting either side know too much of each other's lives. It is hard to be the holder of these secrets, but I have to respect other people's right to privacy.

On one recent visit to Scotland, I spent a holiday with my own son, my adoptive mum and dad and my birth siblings and their children. It was wonderful to spend time with people who not only share my memories, but also look like me. It was thrilling to meet my nieces and nephews and for my son to meet his cousins. We sat down together for meals round a big table and it felt great. I have a dream that one day my entire birth family will sit down together around a table and have a meal together. I now accept this may never happen. Yet, in my mind, the table is set and waiting and there is plenty of room for everyone.

JEANNIE

One evening, when Gordon was about sixteen, we had a meal in an Italian restaurant in the centre of Glasgow. We had been shopping and stopped off for a pizza before taking the train home. It was a Saturday and the streets were full of shoppers. Our table was by the window, overlooking a corner where two busy streets meet. A few feet away from us, a great throng of people swept past us, rushing home as the shops closed. I had been intent on my own thoughts when I suddenly realised Gordon had been silent for a long time – unusual for him as he was a real chatterbox. When I glanced at him, I realised he was silently weeping. It was some time before he could tell me what was wrong.

'Every time I am in the town,' he finally managed to say, 'every time, I see all these people, hundreds of them, I keep looking to see if one of them is my sister or my brother.' He stopped, choking on his tears. 'And the worst bit is, I don't even know if I would recognise them, because I don't know what they look like now.'

He stopped for a while, then began again.

'No, that's not the worst thing, the worst thing is that I don't even know if they are alive or dead. They might as well be dead; I'll never see them again.'

We spoke about his siblings for a long time that night. We took out the photographs and looked at them, trying to imagine how these children would look four years on. I retold some of the stories I remembered of their times together, and he told me stories of being together in their birth family. He related one story I had not heard before. As usual, he had been left alone in the house with his younger siblings. Neither of us knows how old Gordon was at this time, but as the children were all taken into care just before his sixth birthday, he was far too young to be on his own, never mind being in charge of other children. While his parents were out, his sister cut her arm on a broken bottle and he had to run to a neighbour's house for help. When his father came home, Gordon was beaten for allowing his sister to be harmed. I realised he had carried this unfair burden of guilt for over ten years, not speaking about it because he thought it was his fault. Over and over again, I told him how glad I was that he had told me, and reassured him that he was not to blame, that he had been a small child, not responsible in any way. I can't imagine that one discussion lifted the burden, but it was the start of a process of shedding an unjustified sense of responsibility for what had gone wrong.

I told Gordon that night that I could not promise success, but that I would try to find news of his siblings. He was quite clear that he did not want to disrupt their lives in any way.

'I don't even need to know where they are living. They don't need pressure. They have their own lives to lead and I have mine. I just want to know if they are OK.'

It was several months before I managed to contact the other family and spoke to the father by phone. I quickly reassured him that we had no need to see the children or know their address, but that we would very much welcome photographs and updates on how they were doing. He agreed to do so and within a week he had sent us full details of the children's progress. This simple step made a huge difference to Gordon.

As adults, the siblings have all met up with their partners and children and they keep in touch with each other, albeit infrequently. As Gordon said, it is enough to know where they all are, to know that they are well and to share news of their children.

Finding one of his older sisters was a cause of great joy for Gordon and for me. He hopes that in time, the other sister may wish to know him too. Gordon does not remember either of them from his early childhood, as he was a baby when they were adopted. He met them once briefly when he was waiting to be adopted himself, and had pictures of them in his life story book. He often pored over these pictures and talked about the sisters he hardly knew. When Gordon and his sister met on a recent visit to Scotland, we were all astonished at the physical resemblance between them, and at how similar their memories of childhood were. Gordon had always felt himself to be the oldest in his sibling group because of the responsibility he bore for the younger ones, so it was wonderful to connect with a big sister who had spent many years wondering what had happened to her little baby brother.

Knowing how important my own siblings are to me, I am overjoyed that Gordon now has such positive contact with his. They add to his sense of completeness as a person. All of them have been affected in different ways by their early family experiences and some are further along the road to recovery than others, but they all share an understanding of what those experiences were, in a way that no one else can.

13

Moving on

GORDON

Thank you for coming on this journey with me and my mum! Looking back, I can honestly say how lucky I am to have walked this path.

My mum and I chose each other. Now I am grown up, my mum is my best friend and someone I have learned to trust deeply. There isn't a side of me that my mum has not seen, but she loves me just the same and there is not a subject on this earth I can't talk about with her. Even though there have been hard bits for both my mum and me, I would not change the course of my adoption story one bit. I used to wonder what it would have been like to have grown up with a mum and dad, but that is in the past. I would not be the man I am today if my story were different.

It takes a special kind of person to take on the challenge of raising a kid who is not their own. May I, as an adopted child, say thank you to all who have taken on that challenge.

JEANNIE

When I retired from full-time employment, my husband

and I hosted a *ceilidh* for family, friends and colleagues I had worked with across almost forty years and in seven different settings. It was wonderful to bring together so many special people from different parts of my life, many of whom had never met each other before. One of my colleagues gave a speech in which a lot of embarrassing things were said about what I had achieved and the sort of person I had been at work. Afterwards, Gus, one of my adoption sponsors, protested, 'I have never known you in a work context, Jeannie – I don't know about any of the things that guy was saying, although it sounds like it was important work. But as far as I am concerned, the most important thing you ever did was bringing Gordon into our lives.'

I couldn't agree more. I never really had any professional ambitions; I just cared about the kids and the people I worked with and wanted to give of my best – the Calvinist work ethic runs very deep in our family. I think I was promoted more through being in the right place at the right time than through any determined desire to get to the top and earn a large salary. By contrast, adopting a child was a real ambition and something I set about in a very determined way.

We never get to go back and find out what would have happened had we made different choices, but I am confident that if I had not dived into adopting a child, my life would have been much less satisfying than it has been. Perhaps if I had not chosen Gordon, he would have spent the rest of his childhood in care, or perhaps he would have been adopted by a much more competent parent. He seems to be glad he got to choose me! All I know is that the journey was tough, but it has been a good one for us and it is not over yet.

Most parents find it hard to believe their children have grown up. I used to get cross with my mum if she told me I ought to brush my hair and tidy myself up a bit.

'I'm forty, Mum,' I would protest. 'For goodness sake, when are you going to stop nagging me?'

I have to pinch myself to remember that Gordon is almost forty and that I really should stop nagging – if not now, then sometime soon! I make excuses for myself that I do it because he needs a bit more support than most, but I know it is probably just because I am that sort of bossy mum. So I have stepped back quite a bit in the last few years and it has paid off. Gordon keeps in touch with me most days by email and talks to me on the phone more often than the grown-up children of my friends talk to their mums. He is very loving and caring towards us, always asking how his "old folks" are doing. He often urges me to take better care of myself and shows a genuine interest in the detail of our lives. We spend precious minutes of transatlantic phone time roaring with laughter together – it is a very relaxed and happy relationship. I am proud to say he is not just my son – he is also one of my best friends.